The Boxer *and* The Banker

THE
BOXER

AND

THE
BANKER

J. Knox McConnell

VANTAGE PRESS

New York

FIRST EDITION

Published by Vantage Press, Inc.
516 West 34th Street, New York, New York 10001

Manufactured in the United States of America
ISBN: 533-05701-9

Library of Congress Catalog Card No.: 82-90964

To two wonderful women, Mrs. Margarite McFarland Conn, the mother of the greatest boxer in the history of the game, and to Mrs. Marie Rice McConnell, mother of the author: girls, we love you deeply, and, without a doubt, we shall all meet in paradise

Contents

THE BOXER AND THE BANKER: A POEM

A father took a young boy of eight,
  To see a fight between two middleweights;

The kid's father said, "That good-looking boy can fight,
  He's the greatest combination man in the world—a left,
    left hook and right."

As time went on they became great friends;
  No doubt about it, the friendship will last to the end.

At age twenty-one he became a true champ,
  For the boxer made up his mind he would not be a tramp.

Then came the test with Joe Louis one day,
  And after the fight the world heard Louis say;

"Billy's the greatest boxer that I've ever seen,
  He's tough, he's brave, and boy, is he mean."

Of all the fights to have come and gone,
  The greatest of all was the "Louis-Conn."

Then came the war, and what a shame,
  The kid worried about the champ coming back lame;

But the champ returned, and was the kid glad,
  For over four years the kid had been sad.

And now came Korea and the kid was nervous,
  He was really afraid of entering the service.

The champ told the kid not to run and hide,
   For through all the battles he would be at his side.

The kid joined the airborne to fight and to fly,
   He knew with the champ by his side, he wouldn't die.

When the kid came back they continued their relation,
   But the champ kept insisting the kid get an education.

When the kid finished school the champ said, "That's nice,
   For now I'll continue giving you adult advice;

Be kind to all, friendly to many, and close to few."
   These words still echo because they are true.

"Don't ever molest a child, hurt a woman, or go on dope,
   For then I'll turn my back and give you no hope;

But stand up young man for what is right,
   And I don't care how much you fight.

Be quiet, reserved, and don't brag out loud,
   If you do this for me kid, I'll really be proud."

How could I fail with a teacher so bright;
   Frankly, I've always feared his left, left hook and booming right.

In 1962, the kid went down for the count,
   For all his troubles began to mount;

With his father dead, and his mother dying,
   The kid would have given up, but the champ said, "Keep trying."

And now today the kid would like to publicly thank,
   This great champ for helping him start a bank.

In 1965, the champ entered the Hall of Fame;
   About that time, he and the kid became quite tame.

All Pittsburghers know and like to relate
   Why the stories about the champ and the kid are so great.

If you pick on the champ, the kid's by his side,
   If you pick on the kid, forget it, you've just committed suicide.

It's a story for all to get to know,
  Cause with a helping hand you can get out of the ghetto.

This poem is long but bear with me please,
  For now enters that beautiful girl, Mary Louise.

She raised four great kids with her wonderful man,
  Timmy, Billy, Michael, and beautiful Suzanne.

Now back to the kid and the champ once more,
  For this story will be sold some day in a bookstore.

The champ made a statement that sticks in my mind,
  This is really what makes him so good and so kind:

"You see, kid, when you answer the bell for the final round,
  It will depend whether you go up or down,
  By what you did on this ground."

The kid likes to tell of his wonderful life,
  Oh, what an influence the champ, Billy Conn, has had on this
    kid's life.

Acknowledgments

Thanks, Michael, for your genuine help on the manuscript. You're a chip off the old Irish block.

I want to thank the marvelous board of directors and the staff members of the First National Bank, Keystone, West Virginia, for their patience and understanding during the writing of this book. Your help, devotion and loyalty will be remembered forever. After all, this book is written about the greatest boxer that ever lived by the author working for the greatest bank in the United States.

I would also like to thank Dean Kenny, Pat Harris, and Karen Hays, along with the Center for Economic Action at Concord College, for their support and encouragement.

Introduction

Pittsburgh, Pennsylvania, and western Pennsylvania have long been known for their vast and varied sports interest. During a span of about 35 years, western Pennsylvania produced no less than nine world boxing champions. There was no champion more colorful or more widely known than an Irish lad that became one of the truly great boxers of the world. The tough Irishman became not only the Light-Heavyweight Champion of the world, but also fought the greatest fight of the twentieth century. This is the true story of his life, and, more specifically, the impact he had on another Irish kid from Pittsburgh who was ten years his junior. The young man, through the professional fighter's guidance, eventually became president of one of the finest banks in this great United States. The story that is about to be told is true to the most minute detail. This story will tell of the trials and tribulations of both men and how they rose to the top from a very humble beginning. There is no question about the validity of this story for, you see, I was that young man.

Up until the time that Billy came along, the greatest fighter, or the fighter that earned the greatest reputation, was a man from the Garfield section of Pittsburgh, the one and only Harry Greb. Harry was the Middleweight and American Light-Heavyweight Champion. This great boxer fought and soundly beat Gene Tunney, who eventually became the Heavyweight Champion of the world, and Tunney can best be remembered for beating the great Jack Dempsey twice. Every boxer had to fight in the shadows of Harry Greb until the great Billy Conn came along. It is interesting to note that Harry Greb and Billy's dear mother, Maggie, are laid to rest near each other in Calvary

Cemetery in Pittsburgh. I reverently mention the name Harry Greb, for this man truly was the idol of Billy Conn.

You will notice that the chapters are called rounds. I do believe this is the very first time that *rounds* have been used in a book, but I believe it to be symbolic of the life of Billy Conn. The reason for twelve chapters or, even better, twelve rounds is emblematic of the historic Conn-Louis fight for, you see, up through and including the twelfth round, Billy Conn was the Heavyweight Champion of the world.

The Boxer *and* The Banker

ROUND ONE
The Kid Meets the Boxer

Mr. Billy Conn
1715 Denniston Avenue
Pittsburgh, Pennsylvania 15217

Dear Champ:

By now you are well aware that I have painstakingly researched your life and included, from time to time, a portion of my life as it relates to the wonderful association we have had over the years.

Without question, you have been the best friend that I have ever had, and I have always valued your personal advice, thanking the good Lord for having enough sense to heed it. Your kindness to me and the favors that you have extended to me down through the years have made me a much better man, and, above all, a greater American.

I am telling this story with great accuracy, for I have spent two years researching the facts in order to give the reader an accurate account of your great life. All that I say is true, to the best of my knowledge, for I would never lie, being afraid, somewhat, of your very accurate left hook. I'm going to begin, Champ, with our very first meeting when I was eight years old, and at the conclusion of this book, I will complete this letter. Until then, I am convinced that the story about you is simply great for, as I see it along with millions of your fans, you, Champ, are the greatest.

About 4:30 P.M. on the evening of June 3, 1935, my wonderful

1

father informed me that my uncle, Dr. S.H. Holland, was unable to attend a professional fight at Motor Square Garden in Pittsburgh, and he told my mother that rather than waste the ticket, he was going to take me to the fight. My mother objected quite strongly against this because I was so young. My father won out and away we went. All the way to the fight he kept telling me that I would see a young Irish kid fight that had the best combination of punches he had ever seen. My father also informed me that I would see the best-looking boxer that ever entered the ring.

I knew a little about boxers, for a great heavyweight by the name of Charley Massare from Mon City, Pennsylvania, would come to our house because he was my father's friend. Charley was a good-looking boxer who fought all the top contenders. In fact, Charley fought Joe Louis and the fight was stopped because of a cut over Charley's eye. Because of the win over Charley, Joe Louis then became a ranking heavyweight contender.

When my father and I arrived at the Garden, my father gave me the aisle seat. About one hour passed and all of a sudden I felt something on top of my head. I looked up and there was a young fighter with his hands taped up and he was wearing a magnificent robe. I was a bit startled and said to him, "What is your name?"

To which he replied, "I'm Billy Conn. What's your name, kid?"

Before I could tell him my name, he proceeded toward the ring. That night he fought Ray Eberle and won by a decision. After the fight was over, I told my dad that I had to go to the boxer's dressing room. My father asked why I had to do that, and I told him that I never had a chance to give Billy Conn my name. My father got quite a kick out of this and informed me that I could never get into the dressing room. Having never been a bold kid, I told my father he was probably right, but I did not intend to go home without telling the young boxer my name.

All I can say is that God must certainly have been on my side, for as we approached the dressing room, the door was open about four inches and I darted in, ran to the victorious boxer, told him my name and then said, "I'm glad you won, Champ."

Five or six grown men near Billy looked at me and began to laugh. Billy seemed a little startled, but also began to laugh. Little did anyone in the dressing room know, but just about four years later he became the Light-Heavyweight Champion of the world.

To this day, I have never addressed him as anything but Champ;

and, today, whether it be by phone, by letter, or in person, I always sign off by telling him that I love him very much. His determination, spirit, character, and honesty have helped make me a better man. There is no question in my mind that this great and good man had a profound impact on my life.

After our first meeting, I would beg, yell and insist that my father take me to see Billy fight. I would clean my father's car and do anything in the world to be able to hop a streetcar and go down to the gym and watch my hero work out. Incidentally, for washing my dad's Model-A Ford, I received the handsome sum of 25 cents. Billy finally began to recognize me and talk about his upcoming fights. I, of course, was thrilled to death that he would take time out to speak to a poor kid.

I would come home at night and stand in front of the mirror and shadowbox like my idol and try to emulate him in every way possible. Very early in my life, I found something that I did not want to lose and, thinking like a kid, I felt if I could be like him he would like me that much more. Since I was an only child, I felt that I now had a big brother and I never wanted to lose him.

ROUND TWO
Billy the Kid

This truly amazing man was born October 8, 1917 in the East Liberty section of Pittsburgh, Pennsylvania. Billy was the eldest child. He had two brothers and two sisters. His father worked for Westinghouse in Pittsburgh and his dear mother, Maggie, was captain of the household.

At the age of thirteen, Billy, for the lack of something better to do, wandered into the East Liberty Gym, which was on Penn Avenue, across the street from the East Liberty Post Office. The man that ran the gym was a former professional fighter by the name of Johnny Ray; his given name was Harry Pitler and he was Jewish. At this time, it was the beginning of the thirties, the country was in a deep recession, a new president was about to be elected, and the great American people had little to do but hope for the best. When Billy asked Johnny to teach him to box, Johnny said that he felt Billy was one of those tough Pittsburgh kids that was just going to try to steal things from the gym. Billy informed Johnny Ray that he could see nothing worth stealing but tennis shoes and he did not need any shoes. Billy Conn, from childhood on, has always possessed that endearing smile, and I suppose it got to Johnny, for finally he agreed to teach Billy to box; in return Billy had to sweep out the gym and do various things around the place for Johnny. Billy agreed, and a great union developed between the two people.

The kids on the corner all made fun of Billy for hanging around with Johnny and for being what they called the "stooge." The torment was almost too much to bear, but Billy said, "Don't worry about me. One of these days, you will all take notice."

Incidentally, Johnny Ray was one of the greatest teachers in the world when it came to boxing; there was no one better. Johnny Ray

4

knew the Marquis of Queensberry rules and he taught young Billy how to deliver scientifically executed blows, which are called for in order for a fighter to stand up against an opponent. The fighter must know how to deliver a jab, a left and a right cross, an uppercut, and a hook, and be able to attack his opponent's head and midsection during infighting exchanges. No one learned better how to execute those blows than Billy. He also had the ability to avoid getting hit and to keep his hands held high. Johnny kept telling Billy to observe the boxers when they were sparring and to mentally note the fine points of the best boxers in the gym.

Joe Louis later was to say that Billy was absolutely the best boxer that he had ever seen. It's interesting to note that when Billy was told what Joe had said, Billy quipped, "Joe is an honest guy; he never lies." I, too, have taken Joe Louis' word.

In Pittsburgh, there were many gyms for kids to work out in, as well as many arenas that put on boxing matches. In those days, we had Motor Square Garden in East Liberty. There were boxing matches at Duquesne Gardens, South Side Market House, and Forbes Field. Every small town in the area had matches at least on a monthly basis. Today this is difficult to find, if not totally impossible. In fact, I don't know what a young kid would do today if he were in the same position as Billy Conn.

Within a year, Johnny Ray noticed the talent that this tall, lanky kid had and felt that Billy was worth working with. Johnny Ray did a most unusual thing in the very early part of their meeting. Once he noticed Billy's ability, he decided that he should never fight as an amateur, but instead his first fight should be as a professional boxer. Johnny's theory behind this was that you can never learn from an amateur, but you can only learn as a professional. Johnny felt that Billy essentially possessed everything. He was tall, tough, and possessed great, if not blinding, speed.

Johnny Ray was very careful not to rush this handsome Irish kid into the professional ranks until he was ready. Billy's first professional fight was in Fairmont, West Virginia, early in 1935. In this debut, he lost by a close decision. His take was $2.50, and by the time his manager took some incidentals out of his purse, Billy came home with a net of 50 cents.

It is interesting to note that of the first six professional fights that Billy fought, four of them were held in the sister-state of West Virginia. There was no question that Ray began to see the great potential in this handsome kid, for he liked the kid's attitude. Billy was the bullish type, aggressive, and soon Johnny Ray noticed, after the first ten professional fights—of which Billy won seven, that this fighter possessed unlimited possibilities. It is interesting to note, at this point, that Billy's purse went from $2.50 at Fairmont, West Virginia, to over $150 thousand when he fought Joe Louis less than nine years after his professional debut.

Conn's manager learned very early that Conn was a very quick and eager learner, and soon after the first ten fights, Ray developed Conn into a combination man with a lightning left, great left hook, and very accurate right. Ray knew that although Billy, because of his size and build, did not possess a one-punch knockout blow, his lightning-like boxer could improve on his combinations, and, thus, keep from getting hit; after all, the trick in boxing is to avoid getting hit.

Ray taught his star pupil that the closest distance from A to B was a straight line and to jab straight and with accuracy. Ray also insisted that Billy train to perfection and always keep himself in the best of shape. Therefore, with ten professional fights under his belt, Ray began to expand the horizon for this fighter.

After all, he had a kid with a big heart, a kid that liked to fight, a kid that proved he was a true professional by his record, and a kid that was good-looking with a certain charisma that indicated he was of championship quality.

The next ten fights proved to be the turning point of his career. He now was being matched carefully, but at the same time the tempo was being increased by the quality of fighters that his manager was arranging for Billy to fight. Billy had a decisive turning point, which we will go into in another chapter. Of course, one of the turning points for any boxer is to fight and beat a truly great name, for this means not only recognition, but a handsome payday and a chance to become a mainliner on a fight card, and finally the eventual dream of all fighers—first to become a ranking contender and then to have a shot at the division crown.

Billy first began to fight as a lightweight and then moved into one of the toughest divisions in boxing, the middleweight division. I have always called this division the "valley of death," because the middleweights can really fight and, besides being quick, they can hit. If you asked Billy today what the toughest division in boxing is, I have no doubt in my mind that he would say the middleweight is by far the toughest.

One thing remained, however, and Johnny Ray knew it; if you wanted to score a big payday, you had better get your fighter into the heavyweight division. That is where the money was and, in fact, that's where it still happens to be. As of this writing, Holmes and Cooney each received $10 million for one fight. In all the time that Joe Louis fought, I believe the records show that his total gross was under $9 million, and Billy's total purse was under $2 million. One might say that times have changed with the advent of that little box called television.

Meanwhile, Conn always left it up to his manager to choose his next opponents, and Johnny Ray kept picking tougher and tougher fighters and Billy just kept on beating them.

ROUND THREE
Conn *vs.* Apostoli

Absolutely the greatest fight that I ever saw was the second Conn-Apostoli fight held in Madison Square Garden on February 10, 1939. First, however, I must bring you up-to-date on the circumstances surrounding this fight.

On December 28, 1936, Billy fought Fritzie Zivic and won the fight in a grueling ten-round bout in Pittsburgh. Billy received $2,180 for the fight. Those were the days when one could buy a Chevrolet for $600 and a Cadillac for $1,250. This was the beginning of the great career that followed in this great and good man's life. Incidentally, Zivic would go on to become Welterweight Champion of the world by beating the great Harry Armstrong in fifteen rounds on October 4, 1940.

Billy, shortly after winning the fight, went to California for a month. Once there, he offered to fight anyone, but he had no takers. Billy returned home in 1937, and won two fights in a row: one in March and the other in April.

On May 27, 1937, he was matched with the hardest hitter in the middleweight division, a boxer by the name of Oscar Rankins. Billy won a close fight in ten rounds after being knocked down for an eight-count in the eighth round. This was the first time he had ever been knocked off his feet; Oscar Rankins connected with a tremendous right that floored my champion. The ninth and tenth rounds, Billy fought from instinct and won a very close fight.

It's interesting to note that two years later, Joe Louis told him that evidently his manager did not like him or he would not have matched him with Oscar Rankins. In fact, Joe said, "I believe I would think twice before fighting Rankins." But Billy's middle name is fight, and fight he did and winner he was.

8

On September 11, 1934, Teddy Yarosz, a Pittsburgh product, became Middleweight Champion, and Billy and he had some real battles in 1937. Teddy and Billy fought a great fight on June 30, 1937, and Billy won the decision in a twelve-round thriller.

On August 13, 1937, Billy fought Young Corbett III in San Francisco. Corbett had been the former Welterweight Champion, winning his crown February 22, 1933. The fight was a close one, but Corbett won on a decision in ten rounds.

On September 30, 1937, Billy fought Teddy Yarosz again in Pittsburgh, and again, he was victorious in a fifteen-round thriller. Billy said, "I fight no one again until I have my revenge on Corbett."

On November 8, 1937, he and Corbett fought in Pittsburgh and Billy won the fight in a ten-round decision. He gave Corbett a real boxing lesson. Up until that time, he had fought seven times during 1937, winning six out of the seven.

On December 16, 1937, in Pittsburgh, Johnny Ray, Billy's capable manager, matched him with Solly Kreiger, a New York fighter who had everything. He had power, ability, and he was a real professional. Billy lost that fight in twelve rounds, again by a very close decision. Solly went on to become the Middleweight Champion on November 1, 1938.

Because he fought and beat Zivic, Rankins, Yarosz, and made a very credible showing against Kreiger (Billy lost to Kreiger by a very close margin), my champion began to get noticed in New York. You see, up until that time, Billy had fought mainly in and around Pittsburgh. He was a legend in the tri-state area. My buddy was moving along quite well and under the watchful eye of his manager, Billy was really beginning to develop. By now, he could deliver a left jab, left hook, left to the body and a right cross in about two seconds and do it better than anyone he was competing against.

In 1936, he fought nineteen times, winning every time. In 1937, he fought eight times, winning six of the eight. That same year, he had his real test against the best in the Kreiger fight. In 1938, his record was five wins and two losses. He lost to Teddy Yarosz on July 25, 1938, in Pittsburgh, on what I called a very disputed loss.

There was one boxer he wanted, and that was Kreiger. Finally, on November 28, 1938, to a capacity crowd, he gave Kreiger the boxing lesson of his life; my buddy defeated Kreiger in a twelve-round nontitle fight in the same month that Kreiger had won the middleweight crown. Now he was really noticed and wanted by the moguls in New York, the "Big Apple" of boxing.

On November 1, 1938, Fred Apostoli had won the middleweight crown. Fred hailed from the San Francisco Bay area, and he could fight. He, too, had everything, and he was as handsome as Billy. The fight world was clamoring for this match and, on January 6, 1939, to a packed house in Madison Square Garden, the fight was staged. I did not have the privilege of seeing it, but my late father, along with about fifteen hundred other Pittsburghers, went to New York for the fight. You see, this was the first time Billy had fought in New York and in the coveted Garden. The fight was a thriller to end all thrillers, and Billy won on a ten-round decision. He earned his first big payday, $15 thousand, for that fight. The fight was so good that Apostoli, wanting to settle the score, demanded a rematch.

On February 10, 1939, just about one month after their first fight, these two great fighters were again matched in New York and, you guessed it, Madison Square Garden was the place to be. I went to that fight, but here I will digress to tell you how I got there.

First of all, we were poor. I thought we were rich because we had linoleum in every room; I didn't know that you were supposed to have rugs on the floor. Anyway, my dear friend, Fred Seitz, who was about ten months older than I, decided that we just had to see the fight. I liked going with Fred, for if anything went wrong I could blame him, because he was older and also because he was as tough as nails. We decided to tell our parents that we were on a Boy Scout project (Fred finally did become an Eagle Scout), and it worked. I had $12.00 and he had $17.50, and there was no way you could get to New York on that money, so we decided to go to Coulter, Pennsylvania, and hop a freight.

The freight trains always stopped at Coulter to take on water. This particular freight also took us on and it was one hell of a ride. We got into a boxcar and noticed a bum in the corner sitting against the wall. The bum scared me, but after a while he appeared to be quite a nice guy. He informed us that the train was going to Baltimore and not to worry, for he would help us once we got to the yards in Baltimore.

Five hours later, both Fred and I had to go to the bathroom, and I said to Fred, "What do we do now?" Fred asked the bum and he said he also had to go, and he would show us the way. We stepped to the edge of the door of the empty boxcar and with the train going about 60 miles per hour held on to each other and let it go. The bum told us the greatest experience in life is to do this out of a moving train at 60 miles per hour; it was even more exciting to do it at 70 miles per hour. We took his word for it. To make a long story short, the bum helped to get us on a freight to New York and told us he was heading south for the winter. Later in life, I was to feel that this guy had class.

At home, I had typed on a card with my mother's typewriter (mother sold life insurance to help ends meet) the following message: THIS BOY IS DEAF AND DUMB. PLEASE BE NICE TO HIM FOR HE IS MY BROTHER. PLEASE ESCORT HIM TO MY DRESSING ROOM. HE ALWAYS TRAVELS WITH A FRIEND: BRING HIM ALONG, TOO. SIGNED: BILLY CONN. When we arrived at Madison Square Garden, Fred told me the card would never work. I told him to wait and see. Well, we walked up to a guard, and I held the card up and the guard replied, "Gee, I didn't know Billy Conn had a brother that was deaf and dumb. I feel so sorry for that kid." The handsome Irish guard let us in without a hitch. (I used that trick five more times.)

Madison Square Garden was packed to the rafters; it was a well-known fact that Fred Apostoli had come there to fight. What Apostoli may have forgotten was that my hero also came to do battle.

That fight was the best fight that I ever saw. To this day, Billy still says that the second Apostoli fight was the toughest fight of his career. At the beginning of the third round Apostoli stuck his thumb in Billy's eye, and Billy got madder than I ever saw him. For a moment, he just stopped and called him every kind of Italian that there happens to be, and Fred called him a no-good Irish bastard. Finally, the referee stopped the swearing and recommenced the fighting.

In the meantime, Johnny Ray was confused; at the end of each round, he kept splashing water all over his fighter, and as Billy would get up at the sound of the bell, he would slip and fall because of the water in and around his corner. At the end of the tenth round, the fight became very bloody and, again, the thumb went into Billy's eye. When Billy came back to the corner at the round's end, he was furious; he told the people in his corner to get his manager out of the corner, to take the other two "Dagos" in his corner out, and for all of them to go into Fred's corner. He said "Fred's breaking my spine, my manager's confused, and you two are drowning me with the water."

During the eleventh and twelfth rounds, Billy received a terrible

11

beating. His one eye was closed, the other was closing, his eyebrows were cut to the bone, and blood was coming from his nose and mouth. I started to cry, for I was only two rows back, and at the end of the twelfth round, I ran up to the corner and yelled, "Champ, please quit. We'll get him some other time."

Billy was surprised to see me and pointed his glove at me and said, "Sit your butt back down. Don't worry, I'll beat this monkey, and when I'm finished with him, I'll beat your butt for being here. You should be in school, you idiot."

The next three rounds were the best that I have ever seen and Billy sure did give Fred a lesson in boxing and won the decision. He did what he said he would do; he kicked Fred Seitz's butt along with mine.

When Billy came home, he was wrapped up like a mummy. One of the newspapers ran a picture of him with the headline: "IF THIS IS THE WINNER, WHAT DOES THE LOSER LOOK LIKE?" Upon his return from New York to Pittsburgh, Billy immediately checked into the Mercy Hospital to recuperate for seven days. Fred Apostoli did not have a mark on him. He was a good-looking guy that knew how to fight; thus, he made $30 thousand in one month. Boy, did I think that was a lot of money! Billy Conn was now well on his way to becoming not only a household word in this country, but the world now knew about him; the broadcasters at ringside had to duck their microphones under the ring every time the two fighters yelled at each other, for the fight was shortwave radioed around the world.

Fred Apostoli has since gone to his great reward, and after the fight, he and Billy became the best of friends. In fact, Billy always had a very high regard for this magnificient man.

After the second Apostoli fight, the Hollywood Legion Stadium called Billy to come out there and fight. He told them to go to hell. When he was in California, they did not want him; now he did not need them, and he would not go out there for all the money in the world. That's my boy. He always sticks to his beliefs.

For years many people have asked me how it came to pass that Billy Conn finally went to New York, where he eventually took the sports world by storm. I have researched a great deal concerning the reason why Billy eventually arrived in New York and Madison Square Garden. It is well to remember that Billy fought ten consecutive times in Madison Square Garden and won all of the fights.

Every time he boxed at the Garden, he was the mainliner.

Let me reiterate and go back now to December 16, 1937, in Pittsburgh, Pennsylvania, where Billy fought Solly Kreiger. Solly was born on March 28, 1909, and he had a very impressive record, having boxed professionally since 1928. At the time of the first Conn-Kreiger fight, Billy was an inexperienced boxer, and he lost to the great Solly Kreiger. Billy now wanted to avenge this loss. In fact, he used to tell me,"If you think losing is good, you are crazy!"

On November 1, 1938, Solly Kreiger beat Al Hostak in a fifteen-round bout in Seattle for the middleweight crown. Billy wanted so badly to avenge this loss that he offered to fight Kreiger for free. On November 28, 1938, Billy got his chance for revenge, and at Duquesne Gardens, Billy beat Solly in one of the best fights ever in Pittsburgh. Billy won by a decision, and the headline in the paper on November 29, 1938, shouted:

"CONN MASTER BOXER IN BEATING KREIGER."

The very next day, Johnny Ray received the offer from Madison Square Garden in New York to have Billy fight Fred Apostoli on January 6, 1939. I, and many others, too, believe that the real reason Billy Conn became the celebrity that he is today was his boxing the ears off Solly Kreiger and, thus, earning a shot at the very capable Fred Apostoli.

ROUND FOUR
A Correspondence Course in Boxing

In late April of 1941, the entire world knew that Billy Conn, the Light-Heavyweight Champion, was going to fight the great Joe Louis for the heavyweight crown on June 18, 1941. All the kids at the school I attended knew how well I was acquainted with this great king, and a lot of my friends were excited and razzing me about it. In every school crowd, however, there is a bully, and about the middle of May, shortly before school was to end for the summer, this bully kept telling me that Joe Louis would kill my idol. This kept up for weeks, and finally one day, as class was letting out, I told this guy to go to hell. Well, that was all I had to say, for, as you can imagine, he drew a crowd and told me in no uncertain terms that now he would do to me what Joe was going to do to my buddy. Frankly, I was looking for every way out of the situation, but there was no way out of a fight. The bully had quite a reputation for never losing a fight. I looked around for the sympathy of the crowd, but there was none to be found. Off we marched to the railroad tracks with about seventy-five kids following.

The bully's common practice was to beat your head on the rails once he got you down. Of course, this was my main concern. On the other hand, what he did not know was that I saw Billy Conn fight thirty-five times and saw him train for over three-and-a-half years. I knew that my Champ had the best left, left hook, and right combination in the business, so why should I not fight this bully the way Billy fought. You see, up until that time, Billy won all the fights I had seen him in, and usually, he was outweighed. The bully

14

had me in size by twenty or more pounds and was at least two inches taller.

This next part is absolutely true, and it still amazes me. The bully came at me with a tremendous rush and a violent, wild right swing. As he swung, he was off balance and in an instant I thought to myself, "This guy can't fight worth a damn." I hit him just as Billy had hit so many others in the past—with a left, left hook, two quick pumps to the stomach and the hardest right that I ever threw in my life. With that, the fight was over. All the kids told me to give the bully the rail treatment, but I told them I did not do business that way. From that day on, no one ever picked a fight with me, nor did I ever look for a chance to prove myself again.

That night Fred Seitz came over to my house and blabbed it all over the place. I had said nothing, for I knew my mother would give me a beating I would never forget and, when she finished, my schoolteacher aunt would give me another. I was right, for that is what they did.

When my father came home, my mother told him what I had done and what she did to me; my father simply said, "No use beating him again." Later that evening, when I was preparing for bed, my father came into the room, sat on the corner of the bed and told me that had to be the first correspondence course in the history of boxing. Oh, by the way, the bully was quite rough, for as of this writing, he is doing fifteen years in a federal prison.

My penalty for fighting went beyond the beatings from my mother and aunt; I was forbidden to listen to "Gangbusters" and "The Green Hornet" on the radio for one month. Parents were tough on their kids in those days. I found out that it was wiser to avoid a fight than to face my mother's booming right cross, and my aunt's strong left hook.

ROUND FIVE
Conn vs. Louis

Without question, the Conn-Louis fight has to be the all-time best fight ever staged anywhere in the world and, today, there is still so much talk about it that you would think it happened only yesterday.

To set the stage properly, we have to go back in time a bit. In 1937, Joe Louis won the heavyweight crown by defeating James J. Braddock, a gifted boxer, but long over the hill by 1937. During Louis' reign, he was truly magnificent, taking on all comers and simply knocking them out. Truly, there was no greater heavyweight in the history of this country better than the "Brown Bomber," mighty Joe. He possessed great boxing skill, a devastating punch, and he probably had the fastest right hand in the business. From December 1940 through May of 1941, Joe Louis fought every month, and every fight ended in a knockout.

On the other side of the coin, we have the man who would be the capable challenger, a man five years younger than the great champion, a man willing to vacate the light-heavyweight crown in an attempt to wrestle the heavyweight crown from a truly great champion. This young man was none other than Billy Conn.

During the Conn-Bettina fight for the light-heavyweight crown, the broadcast announcer at ringside indicated that the winner of that fight had a very good chance of being matched with Joe Louis. Billy won that fight by a decision in fifteen rounds and became the Light-Heavyweight Champion at the age of twenty-one on July 13, 1939. During his reign as Light-Heavyweight King, he defended his title five times and was successful in each of these encounters.

One thing to keep in mind is that Billy never weighed more than 169 pounds. In fact, there were many fights, which I attended,

16

where Billy never weighed as much as his opponent. He did, however, make up for his size in heart and outstanding boxing ability. Billy Conn was a well-built fighter slightly over six feet in height, but even after he left the middleweight ranks his weight stayed between 165–169 pounds.

The first fight in the light-heavy ranks was for the title Billy won from Bettina. My father strongly objected to Billy's entering the heavyweight division, but Billy told both my father and me not to worry about it. He said the heavyweights were easy to hit, and if you stayed in the middleweight or light-heavy division too long, those guys would break your spine. My father always thought Billy could stay the Light-Heavy Champ until age thirty and then retire gracefully.

There was, however, one thing on Billy's mind—the big paydays belonged to the ranks of the heavies. A top contender for a heavyweight fight would get three times what the light-heavy champ would get. Since Conn had defended his crown successfully five times, he and his manager decided to advance to the heavyweight division and give the young Irish kid a taste of the heavyweight leather. Well, of seven fights, he won them all and four by knockouts.

Mike Jacobs, without question the greatest matchmaker of them all, realized that Conn versus Louis should be a royal battle. First, there was no one else for either boxer to fight. Joe Louis had successfully defended his title against all comers ("bum of the month" as these callers were referred to), and Billy Conn had beaten all the opponents placed in his path. So here you had a truly great champion in the heavy division to fight against a truly great champion from the light-heavy division.

The match was staged for the Polo Grounds and early publicity assured there would be a capacity crowd of 55 thousand spectators. Announcements signaled that seats would sell anywhere from $2.50 to $25.00. The contract signed by the fighters gave Joe Louis 40 percent, Conn 20 percent, and the promoter 40 percent. Paid attendance actually came to 54,500 people, and the gate take amounted to $451,800.

For several weeks leading up to the fight, there was relative calm in both camps. From Conn's side came word that Louis was slow moving, and with Billy's tremendous boxing ability, he could, and would, box rings around Joe. From Joe's camp, there came complete confidence, but they took Conn very seriously. They did

17

predict, however, that Louis would knock out my buddy.

Just two days before the fight, I was delivering papers on a paper route and was hit by a lady learning to drive. Although I did not go to the hospital, I required the attention of a physician and was told to stay in bed for the rest of the week. That got me down, for up to that time I had seen my idol fight thirty-eight times, and he had never lost a fight. I felt that the Irish was giving the Irish good luck. No one was more disappointed than me, for I had looked forward to this upcoming fight with great anticipation, especially since I had a ticket for this fight and would not have to sneak in.

An important consideration surrounding this fight was the fact that Billy's dear mother, Maggie, was dying. She had told her son, just prior to his training of the fight, that she would next see him in "paradise." Billy was so good to his mother, supplying round-the-clock care for her, and this, too, was in the days before Medicare. Billy always said that his mother came first, no matter what the cost.

Many times, the public fails to realize that fighting is a profession and that these men have moments of feeling and love just like the rest of the world. One has only to see Billy holding one of his grandchildren in his arms to see the tenderness of this great man. That's definitely one of the reasons why I love the guy so very much.

On the night of the fight, June 18, 1941, the skies over New York were threatening rain, while the skies over Europe were raining bombs. (As most people know, the war in Europe officially began in September, 1939). On this night, however, the weatherman goofed because it did not rain, and the great fight to be was on. Eddie Joseph was the official referee presiding at this event. The official weigh-in, for the records, showed Conn at 174 pounds and Louis at 199½ pounds. The real truth of the matter was that Conn really weighed 169½ pounds. One of the reasons the promoter listed Billy at 174 pounds was that he was fearful lest anyone should show up contesting the difference in weight. So, my hero was at a weight disadvantage equal to thirty pounds. This was not mentioned before, but Billy was always notoriously slow in the beginning of every fight, speeding up gradually as the fight progressed.

At the start of the first round, both men were extremely cautious. One minute into this round, Louis shot a right and Conn went down. It appeared that Joe had connected, but what had happened was that Billy slipped on water that was in the center of the ring. Joe, being the true sportsman that he was, could very easily have hit Billy on his way down, but, of course, he did not.

18

During the first two rounds, both men showed great respect for each other, but were also wary of each other. These two rounds were awarded to Louis. In the next two rounds, Conn picked up the pace with lightning-like jabs, and he was awarded these two rounds. The following two rounds went to Louis, for he also began to speed up and became very aggressive. Most experts agreed that after the sixth round it appeared that Louis would not knock out Conn, and it definitely appeared that Billy began to become very confident and aggressive. From the seventh round on, Conn displayed the greatest boxing exhibition that any fighter has ever displayed. Conn seemed able to hit the champion any time he so desired, and the champion, in fact, looked somewhat confused. During the second half of the tenth round, Louis made an attempt to rally, but Conn just came back stronger than ever. During the eleventh and twelfth rounds, the challenger just kept coming on stronger and stronger, and staggered Louis in the twelfth round. In fact, during a flurry by the challenger, as Louis hung on, Billy said, "You're in a fight tonight, Joe."

Joe answered, "I know, Billy."

After the short exchange of words the challenger came on again and again with one flurry after the other. Without question, Billy Conn was in complete control of the fight and on his way to becoming the Heavyweight Champion of the world at the age of twenty-three.

Conn's best round was the twelfth, for there was no question that he was well ahead in the fight. Records show that the referee had Conn leading seven to five, one judge had it at seven to four, with one even in favor of Conn, and one judge had it six to six. The press and all experts at ringside had it in favor of Conn, similar to the referee count of seven to five.

At the conclusion of the twelfth round, the handlers in the Champion's corner told him he was behind and his only hope would be a knockout. Louis replied, "I can't hit that kid."

On the other side of the ring, Johnny Ray told Billy to continue to stick him and run, and to keep his combinations going like he had done in the tenth, eleventh, and twelfth rounds. Conn remarked that he was going for a knockout; Johnny Ray violently protested this. Billy knew that he had taken the lead not by back-pedaling but by outfighting the Champ. It was not Billy's nature to win in a retreat, and I am proud of him for the tiger instinct he possesses. He felt he had Louis and was now going to polish him off. Billy decided to continue fighting the great Joe Louis just as he had been doing from the tenth round on—to elude the ropes and keep away from Joe's awesome right punches.

The first two and a half minutes of the thirteenth round were the most exciting in the history of boxing. Suddenly, in close quarters, Louis countered with a hard left hook and a devastating right. Billy sagged, but, like a tiger, attacked Louis with everything he had. In the middle of that exchange, Joe hit Conn with the same combination and that is where the thirty pounds in weight advantage came into play. In an instant, Joe threw twenty or more punches and all but three or four hit their mark; that was the beginning of the end. Billy Conn, up to that time, had never been out and had only hit the deck on one other occasion. Billy was getting back up at the count of eight, but he missed getting to his feet by just one second. Time: 2:58 into the thirteenth round. This fight is regarded by the boxing writers as the best professional fight in the history of the game.

After the fight, Joe Louis said that was the toughest fight that he had ever been in and that he had just faced the best boxer that ever lived. What did Billy say about the champion? He said he was beaten by a truly remarkable man, and he thought that to win he had to out-game Louis, which he almost did. The fight proved to be a great inspiration for both men and, as a result, a friendship developed that was unique. Joe would often say to Billy, "You tried to knock out your buddy, and I had to teach you a lesson."

Several months after the fight, Billy told Joe that he—Joe— should have let him win the title for six months, so he could have told all the guys in the neighborhood he was the Heavyweight Champ. Joe replied, "You had it for twelve rounds and didn't know how to keep it. How were you going to keep it for six months?" Billy and Joe were the very best of friends, and you could see it in their eyes the way they idolized each other.

On June 19, 1946, Conn and Louis were to meet again. But now Billy, age 28, was not the fighter he had been before the war. The years in the service slowed him down, and even I, as a kid, could see that. As predicted, however, the fight was a box office success. This was the first fight in history to offer and sell out $100 ringside seats. Mike Jacobs, the promoter, predicted a sellout crowd which was to be the second all-time great gate. The first being the second Dempsey-Tunney fight. Except for two great rounds by Billy, the fight was not impressive, and he was knocked out by Joe in the eighth round. Joe had slowed down considerably, but he did pack that awesome punch. Yes, I was there at Yankee Stadium that night and knew this was the end of the road for my hero. Billy did make a big payday, however, for his share of the purse was $313 thousand.

He fought and won three additional fights and concluded where his fame began, in an exhibition match with Joe Louis on December 10, 1948. After that exhibition, he hung up the gloves for good. I remember well him telling me, "Well, kid, it's been fun, but it's all behind us now." I concluded that Billy was worn out at age twenty-eight. His boxing career spanned thirteen years of total greatness.

One night, at a banquet honoring both men, the Louis-Conn film was shown and just before Billy hit the deck, Joe yelled out to the crowd, "Bye-bye, Billy." The timing was perfect and the crowd roared. I have the full thirteen rounds on video cassette, and during the writing of this book, I have played the fight back twenty-two times and I would judge it as follows: Conn eight rounds, and Louis four rounds. If Billy had not been knocked out in the thirteenth round, that round very easily could have gone to Conn. Did Conn do wrong by going on the attack in the thirteenth round? I believe not. You see, all great heavyweights seem to be judged by the record of either Jack Dempsey or Joe Louis, and since the days of Louis there has not been one heavyweight that has earned the credit or respect that mighty Joe has earned. In order for Billy to have held his head high in his profession, the only thing to do was to try for a knockout. I have told Billy so many times that maybe he became a greater hero going out as he did than he would have by winning the damn thing. Betting odds on the evening of the fight showed Louis was a four to one favorite, eleven to five to win by a knockout. So I have to say the East Liberty Flash from Pittsburgh didn't do so badly.

Immediately after the fight, Billy wanted a return engagement and promoter Mike Jacobs agreed to it. Jacobs had agreed to give Lou Nova a shot at the title, and he eventually did in November 1941. Well, you know what happened on December 7, 1941, and the return match had to be shelved. Several days after the fight Billy decided to go down to Atlantic City from New York, and while on the boardwalk, was told by the Associated Press that they just received word that his mother had passed away.

That fight on June 18, 1941, brought great fame to Billy Conn and from that night forward his name was known round the world.

The same fight also brought him recognition from Hollywood and the lead in a movie—"Pittsburgh Kid"—in which he played opposite Jean Parker. Billy completed the movie in late 1941, and with our country at war, he decided that he would join the Army. During the making of the "Pittsburgh Kid," Bob Hope and he became friends and their paths were to cross time and time again, both during the service and after the war. It might interest the reader to know that one day I asked Billy what he thought of Bob Hope: "Bob Hope is the first-string quarterback on the premium team of nice guys." I think that's a fine tribute to a truly great American.

My late father said that the twentieth century was split in half by two main events—the Louis-Conn fight and World War II. What was I doing during that memorable fight? Well, I was nursing a very sore arm and leg from being hit by a woman learning to drive, but I hobbled downstairs to our only radio and, obviously, along with the family that loved Billy so much, was quite excited. I'll never forget the end of the eleventh round. My father turned to me and said, "If Billy continues to do what he's doing, he's either going to get knocked out, or we are going to have the biggest party that Pittsburgh has ever had."

Well, we did not have the party, and I cried for two hours. I thought June 18, 1941, was the end of the world for this thirteen-year-old kid. Oh, by the way, the headlines in the paper the next day were as follows:

"LOUIS DEFEATS CONN IN A GREAT FIGHT"

and

"NAZI DECISION TO ATTACK RUSSIA IN 48 HOURS."

In forty-eight hours, they did indeed attack. I don't believe the world has been the same since that day.

Let's look back for a moment in retrospect. Here was Joe Louis, probably the greatest Heavyweight Champion of all time. A 200 pound muscular individual with destruction in either hand; once he got an opening, he never missed putting his opponent away; once he put an opponent down, the man never got back up. On the other side was a tough Irish kid who never weighed over 169 pounds, and who probably possessed the greatest boxing skill of anyone that ever entered the ring. He was not known as a knockout artist, but he was known for being a very clever boxer. Well, what went wrong for Billy that night? After all, he was ahead and probably the first opponent that Louis faced that was completely unafraid. In fact, during the examination of both fighters before the fight, remarks were made as to how slow his heartbeat happened to be. Billy was a notoriously slow starter, and it took him several rounds to really set the pace. He had the knack of making his opponent fight his fight. That is exactly how the fight went for twelve and a half rounds. Joe tried desperately to corner him and body punch him in order to slow the Irish kid down, but it did not work. Billy was too smart and too fast. His fatal mistake, however, was in trying to slug it out with the best hitter in the business. That night had matched, probably for the last time in years to come, two of the greatest fighters in history. I have always said that Billy really became the victor by losing. I know that sounds silly, but even Joe Louis said that without question Conn gave him his toughest fight.

What would have happened if Billy Conn had won that night, either by a decision or by a knockout? Well, I believe he would never have gone down in history as he will go down now. No heavyweight after Joe Louis has ever been recognized as great. They are all branded as so-so. Even Marciano is not rated in the same class with Joe Louis simply because he could not polish the opponent into submission as quickly as mighty Joe. Today, the present champ, Larry Holmes, is asking the world why he is not recognized. He keeps asking, "What do I have to do?" He does not have to do anything, for he will never be ranked like Joe Louis, and for the next fifty years no one will be ranked like him, unless they, too, can finish off an opponent as quickly as Joe and with Joe's style.

Years later, Joe told Billy, "Sooner or later, I knew you were going to try to knock your old buddy out, and I had to fix your ass."

I have asked Billy what Joe's secret was, and he simply said that Joe did not do anything wrong. When he finally got the opening he was looking for, he fired some very quick shots to Billy's head and that was that. You simply could not outslug the mighty Joe. Today, Billy will tell you that you're crazy to think that you can do that and get away with it. Again, I am tremendously proud of the way Billy fought. Being the true sportsman that he is, he told me many times, "I tried to slug it out with the best, and that was my mistake."

What came out of the fight, over and above the purse, was a deep love and affection for these two great champions. Billy attended his funeral, and through an act of dispensation, President Reagan permitted this great champion hero's burial at Arlington Cemetery. What does Billy say today about Joe? Well, he has told me over and over that Joe never spoke a bad word about anyone and that he was a completely honorable man.

On the lighter side, the boys often went to Las Vegas to gamble. Once, at a casino, Joe said, "Lend me $500, Billy, for the crap table." Twenty minutes later, Joe came back to Billy for another $500. After the second $500, Billy told the guys with him that if Joe came back for more money, tell him that he—Billy—left. About an hour passed and Joe came back and asked where Billy was. The guys told Joe that Billy had just left. In fact, Billy was hiding behind a pole. Joe said, "That's too bad. I won and have $3,700 for my buddy."

Billy Conn came out from behind the pole so fast and yelled, "Hey, Joe. I didn't leave. I'm still here."

Another time, again in Las Vegas, Joe and Billy were having dinner and Muhammed Ali came over to their table and told both men what he would do to them if they were now fighting. Joe looked up and said, "If you even had a dream about it, you should wake up and apologize."

Billy spoke up and said, "How would you like to shake that off your ass?—"

With that, Ali turned and said, "You're both crazy."

Incidentally, I asked Billy what he thought of Ali. His answer: "I'm even beginning to think he's the greatest. Anyone that can make $74 million has got to be the greatest." (Combined, Conn and Louis earned a mere $10 million in their careers.)

Billy still insists, however, that Joe was the best. In fact, Billy once told me that if the fighters of the thirties and forties were matched against the fighters of today, you would have to get the Humane Society to protect today's fighters.

Should Billy Conn have been matched at all with Joe Louis? I will always say yes. Billy Conn was a promising and capable challenger, for he had fought and beat twenty *former* world champs and was the headliner ten consecutive times in Madison Square Garden. To my knowledge, this alone is a record. So, why not match the best with the best?

ROUND SIX
Conn vs. Smith

This chapter will certainly be enjoyed by all, for it illustrates that true Irish spirit. The chapter will conclude by showing that Billy Conn's marriage was surely made in heaven.

Due to his tremendous activities in sports, the Champ was destined to run into an extremely tough Irishman by the name of "Greenfield" Jimmy Smith. He was a tough, athletic, professional baseball player who had played in the past for the New York Giants, the Cincinnati Reds, and the Pittsburgh Pirates. Jimmy was a colorful, generous and tough individual. Attesting to his toughness is this remark he made one day when one of the baseball players complained of a pain: he said, "Rub it with a brick." Jimmy never admired weakness, and despite his size, he had no fear of anyone in the world. Smith was also a witty guy. If you were to ask him about someone who was cheap, he would reply, "He's so cheap he wouldn't give you the sleeves of his vest."

One time, while playing in the world series for John McGraw of the world-famous New York Giants, Jim Thorpe, a great Indian athlete, missed a fly ball and McGraw told Smith to tell "that Indian" where to go. Jimmy yelled back to McGraw "Tell him that yourself," he added, "No one tells that big Indian anything."

"Greenfield" Jimmy Smith owned the Bachelor's Club in Pittsburgh, a club enjoyed by athletes as well as businessmen. He wielded considerable influence, maintained a visible profile, and enjoyed political power in Pennsylvania. He was also well-liked. Because of his interest in sports, Billy and he soon became great friends. Jimmy had an unusually handsome family, of which his pride and joy was his beautiful, blonde daughter by the name of Mary Louise. Mary Louise first met Billy when she was fifteen years of age. She was introduced to Billy at her father's summer house in Ocean City, New Jersey. At the very first meeting, Billy fell head over heels for Mary Louise and, in fact, announced to her that he intended to marry her. Mary Louise's response was, "I've heard that fighters get punchy, but at such an early age, and so handsome!" Finally she said, "You're crazy."

Mary Louise was truly a beautiful girl; blonde and stately, she in fact won a beauty contest, being crowned Miss Ocean City.

As the months passed, she started seeing Billy more frequently, but she learned quickly of her father's opposition to Billy, and found herself torn between her father's wishes and her heart. She attended private schools and saw Billy every chance she got. She mastered every skill and possible excuse to get out of the house to see Billy. It is surprising that Mary Louise never saw Billy fight; she did not like the sport. In fact, she always said, "Hitting and hurting people is no sport."

When Jimmy finally realized that the relationship was taking on a serious note, he dispatched Mary Louise to Philadelphia to attend Rosemont College, with specific instructions to Mother Superior to never let Mary Louise see Billy again. Jimmy, of course, was being very protective of his beautiful daughter; stubborn to the end, he refused to accept the relationship and it became a royal battle between two great Irish families.

Once, when in Philadelphia headlining against heavyweight contender, Gus Dorazio, Billy sent Mary Louise twenty ringside tickets. The sisters, under strict orders from Jimmy, barred Mary Louise from going to the fight. When Billy was introduced, he looked around and saw the empty seats and he was heartbroken. He almost lost the fight.

One week after the Louis fight, Billy's mother passed away and on her deathbed she told Billy to marry Mary Louise. She said the marriage would be a good one and would be everlasting. One day after the funeral, Billy and Mary Louise ran away and got married in St. Patrick's Church in Philadelphia—without Jimmy's permission.

In March, 1942, Billy entered the Army. Soon after, his first son, Timmy, was born, and Billy came home on leave. After the christening ceremony, Billy's new father-in-law asked him to come over to his house. Billy thought the invitation was to toast the baby. When he arrived, Jimmy was in the kitchen, scowling. Jimmy remarked, "I can lick you, and you're afraid to try me."

Billy answered, "I'm afraid of no one."

At that moment, Jimmy hit Billy with a right. In protecting himself, Billy broke his left hand. Art Rooney, president of the Pittsburgh Steelers, was there, and he stepped in and broke up the fight; he had to pull Smith away from Billy. Billy later remarked, "Why is it that people always grab and hold me instead of the other guy? They hold me and let the other guy continue to hit me!" The ironic part of this tale is the fact that Joe Louis had decided to fight Billy again for the world title: because of his hand, Billy was unable to take on Joe Louis for the title. This was Billy's first and only amateur fight which, I conclude, was a draw.

The beautiful part of this father-son relationship began in 1950 and lasted until the death of Jimmy Smith. They were great friends and every Sunday Jimmy was at Billy's home for Sunday dinner. I have always said, being an Irishman myself, that the Irish love to fight and they fight for love. Jimmy helped guide Billy and Mary Louise to a sound financial reward. He insisted that the young couple invest in rental properties and a nice home. Through his guidance, they did just that.

The love affair between Mary Louise and Billy is still going strong, and it will never stop being so. They have produced four beautiful kids: Tim, Billy, Michael and Suzanne. All are quiet, reserved, and lovable kids. Because of my association with Mary Louise and Billy, the Smith family members, including Mary Louise's wonderful mother and her brother Jimmy, are close friends of mine.

Every single time he saw Billy, to the very day he died, Louis would tease Billy: "Is your father-in-law still kicking the shit out of you?"

ROUND SEVEN

The Champ
Goes to Hollywood

Several months after the fight of the century, Mr. Arthur Yates, head of Republic Studios, called Billy and said he would like to discuss a Hollywood career with him. Billy's good looks and splendid figure, along with the historic Louis-Conn fight, indicated to Mr. Yates that this man could possibly become a motion-picture actor.

Billy and Mary Louise got on a train and the next stop was Hollywood. When they arrived in the film capital, Bob Hope, already a friend of Billy's, threw a splendid party at his home for the Pittsburgh boxer. Many stars were there to greet the Champ and his beautiful wife. In the center of the reception area, Bob Hope had a huge cake made up like a boxing ring. In one corner there was a figure of Billy and in the other corner one of Jimmy Smith, and the referee was a small representation of Mary Louise. Bob Hope knew quite well that Jimmy Smith did not like Billy at that time, and this staged cake really broke Billy up.

Billy took a screen test and passed it with flying colors. (Mary Louise also passed a screen test, but Billy would not let her get involved.) As mentioned before, he was given the title role in "The Pittsburgh Kid," a legendary story about a boxer called Kid Tinsel.

Working on the script eight or more hours a day, everything was soon ready. The first day on location in Hollywood, Billy had to sit in the makeup chair and the minute the makeup staff began to put lipstick and rouge on him, he came flying out of the chair and said, "I quit." Well, the studio went wild. They argued that he had signed a contract and was given $25 thousand, and that he could not quit. After many hours of persuasion, he finally agreed to begin shooting. His leading lady was the beautiful Jean Parker, a real pro. Up until that time, the only acting my buddy had done was thumbing his nose to the audience in Madison Square Garden during the Lee Savold fight. Understandably so, the acting was quite rough for Billy. He rehearsed for two weeks with the camera crew shooting around him. The movie was completed in the total time of about three months. Today, the movie can be seen every so often on the Late Show.

Billy did a very credible job and so was asked to play the leading part in "Gentleman Jim," the story of James J. Corbett, the former Heavyweight Champion of the world. Billy declined the part, for he wanted to return to his people and the city he loved so much, the one and only Pittsburgh. Errol Flynn was finally chosen to do the part.

Incidentally, Mary Louise could have had a part in either movie, and often she has told me she regrets not doing so, for she would have liked her children and grandchildren to have been able to see it.

I always tell Billy he was robbed for not getting an Oscar for his part and he quickly replies that I'm "nuts." Just recently, I wanted to secure the film and show it to our friends, but Billy said he would burn it and give me his lightning-punch combinations. Needless to say, I did not get the film.

Billy Conn's ideas about Hollywood were simple. He liked the people and the area, but Pittsburgh was his home and he wanted to return. Even today, he very seldom strays from home. On my vacations from the bank, I have been able to persuade him to go to a few places with me, but he always says, "Come over to the house, kid, and let's watch TV." It does not matter where we are just as long as I'm with Billy. We enjoy each other wherever we happen to be.

Billy always tells me how happy he was in Hollywood, and one day the great John Wayne came over to his location and gave him a word of encouragement. Billy loved the people that he worked with and has fond memories of Hollywood, not to mention the $25 thousand he received for his part in "The Pittsburgh Kid."

Billy was so handsome that while in Hollywood the great actor, Alfred Lunt, said that Billy had to be the best-looking man he ever saw. There is no question about it, Billy Conn, if he so desired, could have been one of Hollywood's leading male actors.

ROUND EIGHT
The Champ Goes to War

In March of 1942, World War II was in full bloom and our country was heavily involved in the conflict. The Champ, at this point, was undecided as to what branch of the service to join, for it was inevitable that he would be drafted to serve in the Armed Forces.

In New York City there were several recruiting offices and Billy visited the Navy office to discuss its program.

A commander recognized him and said, "You are to go into the Navy, and you are to go in right now!"

The Champ wanted to know why the commander had singled him out. The latter said, "Gene Tunney, the former Heavyweight Boxing Champion of the world, has just been made an officer in the Navy and put in charge of all sports figures entering the service."

Because the commander was ordering the Champ to go immediately into the Navy, the Champ, with his usual wittiness replied, "Tell Tunney that Billy Conn is not about to wear those funny pants, and I'm not about to become a 'Tunney' fish."

The commander told Billy that the admiral, through Tunney, wanted Billy in the navy and Billy would not have to wear those funny pants. Tunney, for some reason, said that he did not care what anyone said, Billy Conn was going into the Navy and he *would* wear those funny pants. Billy finally told the commander pretty much what he could do with the Navy.

With that, he left the Navy Recruiting Office and went down one flight of stairs to the Army Recruiting Office. He told them he was Billy Conn and he wanted to enlist and serve his country—anywhere his country wanted to send him. The Champ said, in his usual joking manner, "Why not make it Staten Island." Ironically, that is exactly where they sent my buddy. After a few months, however, he was sent to Jefferson Barracks, Missouri.

The army had plans and asked the Champ to organize a boxing team to go to Europe, and since Joe Louis had already entered the army, he was also asked to organize a boxing team to depart for England. Billy spent eighteen days on the water and finally arrived in Liverpool, and then on to a replacement depot at Stone, England.

Then a strange thing happened. All the soldiers in his particular company were sent to a rough and tough sergeant at the replacement depot who was telling the recruits, in a manner that only a sergeant can, that if anyone thought they could lick him, let them step forward. Billy, of course, took that step forward.

The sergeant asked his name. To which the Champ replied, "Billy Conn. Let's see how well you can fight!"

With that, the sergeant took a step backwards and said, "I will fight any man but him!"

He whispered to Billy in a low tone that he had to give the recruits this "crap" to keep them in line. "Now is there anything I can do for you?" he asked.

Billy answered, "Sergeant, I have not had an egg in a month."

Within fifteen minutes, a dozen eggs were scrambled for Billy, and he and the sergeant became good friends.

When Billy organized his boxing team in the service, he instructed the team to put up a good fight against the other teams, but not to hurt the officers. After all, they were the ones who gave them cigarettes. Jokingly, Billy said, "They must also be involved in the 'black market' and we can get a lot of stuff from them."

From time to time, Billy put on exhibitions and there was one instance when a man named Costello Cruz wanted to box Billy. Cruz said he was going to fix this good-looking guy once and for all. In the first round, he hit Billy so hard that he knocked him out of the ring.

Billy climbed back into the ring and said, "Now you're going to get the beating of your life, because I'm going to hit you with everything—even 'Hitler's' mustache!"

The referee moved to stop the fight and Billy said, "If you stop this fight, I'll turn on you and give you the same thing!"

The referee stepped back and witnessed a tremendous boxing lesson.

About the middle of 1944, when the war was winding down,

Billy ran into his good friend, Bob Hope, and asked him if he could go on tour with Hope and Jerry Colonna. Hope arranged it with the proper people and Billy went on tour with the Special Service Forces until the end of World War II. His total time in the service was approximately three-and-one-half years.

Once, Billy and a full complement of soldiers were on board a C-47 that had a locked elevator. The pilot got the plane off the ground by using power, but he immediately told the passengers of the problem. They were told to get into the tail section and brace themselves. Billy led the group in prayer and said to himself if he got out of this fix he would give his church in Pittsburgh a $5,000 statue of the Blessed Mother. Well, the plane landed without incident and Billy immediately sent a check to the priest for $5,000.

Another time, he was with Bob Hope and they ran into a storm in the south of France. Billy began to mumble something and Bob Hope asked him what he was doing.

Billy replied, "I'm praying."

At that, Bob Hope said, "How about including me in that prayer!"

Billy's wit shows up again and again; when the soldiers were returning to New York, he told them to go to Toots Shor's restaurant and tell Toots that he—Billy—sent them down for a free dinner and drinks. When Billy came back and entered Toots' restaurant, Toots was furious.

Toots yelled, "you 'crumb bum.' All you've done this past year is to send broken-down soldiers to my place and tried to break me."

This, of course, is Billy's form of humor.

When he was in the service, he and Joe Louis would run into each other from time to time. Joe told Billy, "You should be glad you did not get into the Navy since Gene Tunney did not like you. He sent Barney Ross, Ken Overlin, and Gus Lesnivich to the South Pacific and Billy Soose to Alaska. He would have sent you so far away that an eight-cent postcard could not have reached you." In those days, a postcard cost one cent.

In no way did Billy Conn ever discredit the U.S. Navy, but due to the fact that Gene Tunney made unreasonable demands on him, he chose a better route and that route was the Army. He would have gone any place in the world for the American people because he is truly a great American and a model soldier.

ROUND NINE
A Funny Thing Happened on the Way to the Fight

This chapter is intended to point out some very funny things that occurred in Billy's life. First of all, Billy is truly a funny guy with a great sense of humor, and he is just a delight to be with. When Billy started hanging around with Johnny Ray, all the local kids on the corner used to call him "The Matzo Runner," and Billy, of course, would reply, "Don't worry about me and Johnny."

Billy and Johnny never had a contract, but in order fo fight in New York, a contract was required. Prior to that, Billy simply gave Johnny one-third of all he took. All the lawyers would go broke if it were left up to Billy and Johnny. When Billy hit the big time (after the second Apostoli fight), everyone in New York said that he should drop Johnny Ray. Billy's comeback remark was that Johnny knew more about boxing than all other fight managers and that he would never think of replacing Johnny as his manager.

One day Billy got a call at his home in Pittsburgh and it was the "rag man." This infamous character was known for stealing the finest men's suits from the best stores in Pittsburgh and Chicago. On this particular day, the "rag man" got caught. (Billy had bought some beautiful suites from him at half price and I had also purchased two blue suits from him. Billy always said the "rag man's" overhead expenses were low and profits were high.) Anyway, the "rag man" got caught in Pittsburgh and was scheduled to appear before an Allegheny County judge. He needed a character witness and called "Uncle Billy."

When Billy walked into the courtroom, the judge called him aside and said, "The moment I saw you enter the courthouse I knew the 'rag man' was guilty."

Billy replied, "Let him go, Judge. After all, the stores he took the suits from have been robbing the public for fifty years."

The judge told him to get out.

Then Billy dropped a bomb on the judge; he leaned over to the judge and whispered, "What size to you take, your Honor?"

And the judge replied, "If you and the 'rag man' don't get out of here, I'll put you both in the slammer."

One time, Billy was fighting the fight of his life against a real hitter that outweighed him by thirty-five pounds. The fighter was the capable Lee Savold, a good heavyweight, and the fight was in Madison Square Garden. After the fifth round, the audience began to clap for more action. Billy moved in on Savold, and Savold gave him a shot to the head that almost fractured his skull, then a shot to his nose that broke Billy's nose, and then a shot to his ass that almost broke it. Billy turned to the audience and thumbed his nose, and then began to box, but no more would he move in close to Savold.

Billy won the fight easily in twelve rounds. Just prior to the fight, Johnny Ray asked for 42½ percent of the gate. Mike Jacobs told Billy he would give him 40 percent or there would be no fight. Billy told Jacobs, who was probably the best fight promoter that ever lived, one word, "Good-bye," and walked out of his office.

The next day Mike called him and said, "Okay, you and your manager have your 42½ percent, but I want a good fight."

Billy said, "You'll get it." Uncle Mike got a good fight and made money to boot.

Of all the fighters that Mike Jacobs promoted, there is no question in my mind that Joe Louis and Billy Conn were his favorites. The reason I say this is because I'm sure they were the only ones invited to his home. One time in Las Vegas, when Jack Kennedy was seeking the nomination for the Presidency, Billy was doing some public relations work for the Stardust Casino. He was there at the casino when the loudspeaker began to page him. When Billy arrived at the paging station, Jack, Bobby, and several of their friends were already there. They knew Billy and wanted good seats for the show. During their conversation, Billy told Jack Kennedy that he would make sure his close friend, David L. Lawrence, governor of Pennsylvania, would be on his team.

Jack said he was worried that the governor may not be for him;

he said, "Are you sure you can swing him our way?"

To which Billy replied, "If I tell you a chicken can pull a freight car, hitch his ass up."

Jack Kennedy had never heard that one. Billy made his promise a reality and David L. Lawrence was indeed for Kennedy; he eventually received a Cabinet-level job in the Kennedy Administration.

About a week before Joe died, Billy and another man went to see him. Joe could not speak, but he could hear. The fellow with Billy said, "All you need is a nineteen-year-old girl, Joe."

Billy replied, "Joe, if he saw a nineteen-year-old girl he would keep her for himself." Joe laughed at that.

Exactly eight years after the kids razzed Billy about hanging around with Johnny Ray, calling him the "Matzo Runner," Billy walked into Nick the Greek's bar in East Liberty, Pittsburgh, and gave Nick $1,000 cash and said, "All the guys that razzed me for eight years—get the bastards sick and drunk for a month and tell them it's from both the 'Matzo Runner' and the Light-Heavyweight Boxing Champion of the World." Shots of liquor were fifteen cents in those days. Sure enough, Nick poured the liquor and the guys got drunk.

Determination was the middle name of this great champion. I told Billy that I should be a boxer, and he told me to get an education. He said, "Don't you realize how terrible this business is? It's not the punches that are bad; it's the fact that you can't go with girls when you are in training." He asked me, "What is worth that?" According to Billy, it's the only business in the world that prevents you from going with girls.

We had an old fighter in our neighborhood by the name of Chris "Cuddy" DeMarco who was great in the early 1920s. One day I asked Billy what in the hell was wrong with him. Cuddy sold shirts at five dollars apiece. I asked "Cuddy" if he had any specials and he replied, "Yes, I have a special sale, two for ten dollars." Billy told me that "Cuddy" won 161 fights in a row and fought five times a week.

Billy said, "Hell, you can't fight 161 girls in a row without going goofy."

One day I said to Billy, "You don't look well. What in the hell is wrong?"

He told me, "I have not eaten for six weeks and have lost 39 pounds."

Billy told me that when he was down the street five guys had mistaken him for his brother Jackie (Jackie weighed 250 pounds). Billy ran home, swearing that was the last straw. He went from 215 to 176 pounds and has never gained weight again. I think this discipline is a real tribute to his character.

One time we were in the Bahamas together and a cab driver in his early sixties kept looking at Billy and, finally, he said, that Billy looked familiar. Billy said, "I'm Joe Louis' cousin."

The cab driver immediately said, "Oh, you're Billy Conn."

There are so many stories that they alone could fill a book, but I would like to relate one that is priceless. After he fought Joe and received his check, he went to the Mellon Bank in Pittsburgh. He had newspapers under his arm and said he wanted all the money in bills. Nine vice-presidents came running to talk him out of it, but he said, "I want my money. The check is good, isn't it?" Well, after some talking, they gave him the money, and he walked out of the bank with the money in his newspapers. The nine vice-presidents looked in amazement as he walked out of the bank with $150 thousand in bills.

One day I was with Billy and a sportswriter was interviewing him. When the sportswriter asked what he was doing now, Billy replied, "Nothing." (Billy has income from a very large apartment building, plus Social Security).

The reporter kept asking him over and over again, "You mean you are not doing anything?"

And Billy replied, "Listen, boy, only a horse is supposed to work and even the horse turns his ass to the job." The reporter didn't ask him again what he was doing for a living.

Billy won the light-heavyweight crown on July 13, 1939, by outboxing champion Melio Bettina. A return match was set for September 25 of the same year in Pittsburgh. Just two days before the return match, Billy looked outside his house to discover that his new Cadillac was missing. He soon discovered that his brother, Jackie, a pretty fair middleweight fighter, had borrowed the auto without the Champ's permission. Billy immediately offered a $300 reward for Jackie's whereabouts. Late that afternoon, Jackie returned and replied that there was a $300 reward for the return of the car, and he was there to collect the reward. Billy marched Jackie to the garage and said, "Your only reward will be my left hook."

With that, the battle began. Fifteen minutes later, Jackie finally said, "Okay, get it over with." Billy promptly obliged with a smashing right to Jackie's jaw. Just then a car full of cops broke into the garage followed by the famous fight promoter, Mike Jacobs, and Billy's manager, Johnny Ray. Billy was smeared with Jackie's blood and Jacobs asked if Billy was hurt. Billy insisted he was okay.

Jackie, however, was not. He cried, "What about me?" With that, Jacobs began kicking Jackie in the ribs.

Billy finally spoke up, "Can't two brothers have a little fight?"

Jacobs replied, "Yes, but not twenty-four hours before one brother has to defend his Light-Heavyweight title."

Billy replied, "Don't worry, I'll win." And he did.

In 1940, a few days before Billy's first heavyweight fight with Bob Pastor, Billy was looking out of the window of promoter Mike Jacobs' office, which was on the sixth floor at the corner of Broadway and Forty-ninth Street in New York. Down below on the street was Jimmy Johnston, Bob Pastor's manager. He noticed that Jimmy would thrust his hat out to make a point. Billy could not resist the chance and dropped a paper cup full of water right into Jimmy's hat. Billy then beat a hasty retreat down the stairway. Conn went on to knock out Pastor in the thirteenth round.

Another time Billy and Harry Krause, a very credible middleweight, were staying in a hotel together. As both men were preparing for bed, Harry noticed from the reflection in a mirror that Billy was hiding his money under the mattress. Harry asked Billy why he was doing that since both men were friends and they were not leaving the room. Billy turned to Harry and replied, "Harry, there are thieves in this room."

I was watching Billy train in the gym one day, and he was punching the bag so fast, without missing a beat. I asked him how he could do it so easily and gracefully. He answered, "Nothing to it, kid. You see, it doesn't punch back." With that, he gave me his famous laugh.

One time Billy and I were attending a professional fight and one of the boxers, before the fight, blessed himself. I leaned over and asked Billy if that helped. Billy quickly replied, "Yeah, it helps if you can fight."

In the midsixties Billy was asked to referee a fight in Mexico City, Mexico. The hometown favorite received a serious cut over his eye and Billy, using good sense, stopped the fight. That action started a riot and the mob wanted to hang Billy. They pelted him with everything they could pick up. The soldiers arrived and formed a path so that Billy could make a quick exit. Halfway out of the arena, Billy turned to a guy and asked, "What do I do when the soldiers run out?" Billy escaped; however, he had bruises all over his sides and back. Just two days later a mob in the same city lynched three soccer referees. I call Billy every once in a while and ask him to go to Mexico with me. He quickly tells me what I can do with Mexico. This international incident earned Billy a spot on the Johnny Carson Show.

One Thanksgiving Day when Billy was the Light-Heavyweight Champion, he and his father got into a fight. They went out back, and his brother took sides with the father. While they were fighting, Jackie came along and sided with Billy. Well, a battle royal developed. After the fight father Conn said, "Let's all go in and eat the turkey." When Jackie started in the house his father stopped him and told him he was not invited into the house since he had been on Billy's side; Jackie did not eat turkey that Thanksgiving.

One day the renowned veteran actor of stage and screen, Harold Gary, was taking Billy to see a film about the life of Mozart. As they were going to the theater Billy asked, "Harold, how many fights did he win?"

Harold jumped into the air and said, "Billy, Mozart was one of the finest composers of music the world has ever known! He was not a fighter!"

With that Billy said, "Harold, you go and see the life story of Mozart. I will meet you back at the hotel!"

ROUND TEN
The Champ Advises the Kid

I very seldom did anything without talking it over with Billy. After I came out of the service and went to college, my maturity showed me that he was a bright individual and a great philosopher.

I told BIlly one day that I would like to follow in his footsteps, but he soon told me not to be a fool and to get a good education. In fact, his very words were, "Go to college, kid, and get some of those fancy letters after your name. That way you'll have something forever." I once told him that I did not think he had done very badly. After all, he had a home worth well over $150 thousand and an apartment building worth about $400 thousand. He replied wisely, "For everyone that makes it, ten thousand don't." I went to college and got that fancy set of letters after my name (Bachelor of Science) and then had to look for a job.

I went up to see the Champ one night and told him I was really mixed up; I didn't know what to do. Out of the clear blue sky, he said, "If I were you, kid, I would be a banker. They go to work at 9:00 A.M. and leave at 2:00 P.M. and all day long they sit and look at the most wonderful stuff in the world—money." I told him that I knew absolutely nothing about banking and he said, "Neither did those monkeys before they went to work in a bank." He informed me that he did not know how to box until he was taught. I asked him if I could give his name as a reference and he said that I certainly could.

That night, as I left his home, I turned and said, "Champ, you always come through when I need you."

He laughed and said, "Kid, when you use my name, you'll either get the job or get shot."

I applied to three large banks in Pittsburgh and, within a week, Peoples First National Bank (Pittsburgh National) called and I was hired for the credit department. Billy's name had worked like a charm. In fact, the president of the bank at the time, Mr. Robert C. Downie, had the greatest respect for Billy and every time Mr. Downie and I saw each other he would tell me to say "hi" to the Champ.

Several years went by and I soon had an offer to go with a bank in Oil City, Pennsylvania, and again I talked to my buddy. After about a three-hour talk, Billy said, "Take it. Although it's a small bank, you can now be a complete banker by learning everything about a bank; on the contrary, at the big Pittsburgh bank you are only learning one aspect of banking."

I truly regretted leaving the bank in Pittsburgh, for it is one of the finest banks in the country, and it meant leaving many friends behind. Even today, I keep in contact with that bank because its staff members and its general character are simply great. I traveled to Oil City and again spent about two years in another fine bank. One day the state auditors came in and informed me that a bank in Indiana, Pennsylvania, the home of actor Jimmy Stewart, was looking for someone to institute an installment-loan department. On the weekend I went down to Pittsburgh and told the Champ about it. He again said, "The greatest experience is doing." He wished me Godspeed, and off to Indiana, Pennsylvania, I went.

Several years passed and Billy and I kept in contact; either we would phone each other or about every two weeks I would travel the fifty miles to see my parents and Billy. Finally, I had a most unusual opportunity to manage a $34 million savings and loan association located only about 150 yards from where Billy lived. I did not know what the job paid, or what my duties would be, but I would once more be back with the man I liked more than any one in the world. In fact, I did not even tell Billy about it. I accepted the job in late 1958. In the meantime, while in Indiana, Pennsylvania, I had thoughts of starting a bank. I felt that working for someone forever might not be the best thing for me. I felt, however, that I was still young and could continue to work for someone to gain the needed experience. My days at the savings and loan were very happy days, but I kept on thinking about starting a commercial bank. I told Billy about it, and he said he would do anything that he could to help me.

In early 1960, with the full knowledge of the officials of the savings and loan, I applied for an application for a state charter in Blairsville, Pennsylvania. Blairsville is a rural community in Indiana County about thirty-eight miles due east of my beloved Pittsburgh. The Democratic Party was in power and, having asked for Billy's help so much in the past, I decided to try to do this with the help of a couple of other people. The application began to move along quite well and after about eighteen months it looked like the new bank would become a reality. In late 1962, an injunction was issued restraining the banking commissioner from issuing the authority to open, although he had given us his consent. In November, the democratic candidate for governor was defeated and the republicans came into power. On December 28, 1962, my father suddenly died in the office of the Mayor of Clairton, Pennsylvania. I did everything in my power to have the injunction lifted, but it was to no avail. In the meantime, I had sold stock, purchased a building, began to hire personnel to run the bank, thinking that once the banking commissioner gave his consent nothing else mattered. But I was dead wrong. The injunction did matter, since only the Pennsylvania Supreme Court could lift the injunction. What chance did a 180-pound, six-foot Irishman have against the other banks that were protesting my chance to make a living in a free country?

By now, you can imagine what I did. You're dead right; I went to see the Champ. I related to him the spot I was in and that I had found out the presiding judge was Chief Justice Bell and that his brother was Bert Bell, the National Football League commissioner. I told Billy the only chance that I had was to get to someone in the supreme court that would look upon my case fairly and impartially. I then asked Billy if he would call Art Rooney, president of the Pittsburgh Steelers, for I felt the only chance I had in this world was to see if Mr. Rooney would intercede on my behalf. After listening to me for a full hour and not saying a word, this is exactly what the great Billy Conn said to me, "Kid, it looks like you're on the ropes. I won't call Art Rooney for you, but I'll take you right now to see him." Ladies and gentlemen, how in the world could I not love Billy Conn?

We went down to see Mr. Rooney at the Steelers' office in the Pittsburgher Hotel, and Billy told me to repeat my story exactly as I had told it to him. I told Mr. Rooney about my entire life and what the charter in Blairsville meant to me. After a while, Mr. Rooney sat back in his chair and said, "Young man, something like this cannot be fixed and I can tell you now I would not fix anything even if I could, but I do believe you are worth working with. Now leave me alone and let me see what I can do." I told Mr. Rooney I did not want anything fixed for I, too, did not work that way. I just wanted a fair deal. Billy told Art about our friendship and that I had never lied to him. With that, we left Mr. Rooney's office.

On the way back to Billy's home, I asked Billy what he thought and finally he looked at me and laughed. After he laughed, he said, "How are you going to beat three Irishmen? Don't worry. I'm sure everything will be all right." Billy reminded me of something that I will never forget. He said, "If you get the damn bank that you want so much, don't vent any anger on the people that opposed you. For if you get it, then you are the Champ." He told me that he always kept his temper in the ring, because when you lose your head, your ass goes with it.

Exactly fourteen weeks later, the Pennsylvania Supreme Court ruled in my favor on the basis that if the banking commissioner of Pennsylvania ruled the granting of a charter then no one had the power to stop it. In mid-October of 1963, the Conemaugh Valley Bank opened for business. I asked Billy what I could do for him and he replied, "Get me fifty pounds of ten-dollar bills, kid, or if you can't do that, then I'll take a steak dinner instead." We settled on the steak dinner.

What a guy this Billy Conn happens to be. A man like Billy will only come through my life once. I respect that gifted man and will never violate this personal friendship. A true test of friendship is knowing the other person is there if you need him, but not using that friendship in any way other than honorably. Billy Conn is absolutely the reason I have stayed in banking, claiming this field as my chosen profession.

In 1972, I got the bright idea of writing a book entitled *How to Borrow Money* so I bounced it off Billy and he said, "By all means do it, for we should put something back in our lives that we have gained from our experiences." After the book was released, he called me one day and said he thought I had made a mistake. I asked him what he meant and he said, "I've been sitting here thinking that your book title should have been *How to Repay A Loan*. He said with a title like that I would sell millions. That's my Champ; not only quick on his feet, but amazing with his comebacks.

I eventually sold my interest in the bank because an offer came forth that appeared loaded with a chance of a lifetime—to be consi-

dered as an international banker. The position was with the government on the island of Saipan about 120 miles north of Guam. The
job: to start a development bank. You guessed it; again, I sat down
with the Champ and he said, "Take it for a couple of years because
it appears to be right down your alley, and it will give you the
opportunity of traveling through the Pacific that you just couldn't
do any other way."

In June 1975, I departed for Saipan where I became president
of the Micronesia Development Bank. This was the greatest single
experience I have ever had in my life. I thought the service was
exciting, but Saipan had it beat by a mile. Two years had elapsed
and when I wrote to Billy about how much I missed him, he said,
"Think it's time to come home."

I came home on July 1, 1977, and went to work in the southern
part of West Virginia. Billy came down to the bank, which is about
250 miles south of Pittsburgh, and after a few minutes informed me
that he thought the place was great, and that we would not be too
far away from each other. Then he said, "Kid, this is it for you for
the rest of your life, because I do believe you are happy and con-
tented." Billy has gotten to know our directors and staff members,
and he loves them as much as they love him. So this is where I
shall remain with truly a great bank and wonderful people. Over
the past five years, we have won five awards for excellence from
the business community of southern West Virginia. Just recently,
our bank had the honor of becoming the first bank in West Virginia's
banking history to be awarded a branch. So, as of this writing, all's
well with the world. Thank you, Champ, for your devout interest
and confidence in me.

Joe Louis and Billy Conn slugging it out, toe-to-toe, in the thirteenth round of the famous Louis-Conn fight, June 18, 1941. *UPI photo*

Billy Conn connecting a hard right to Joe Louis' head in the eleventh round of the Louis-Conn fight. *UPI photo*

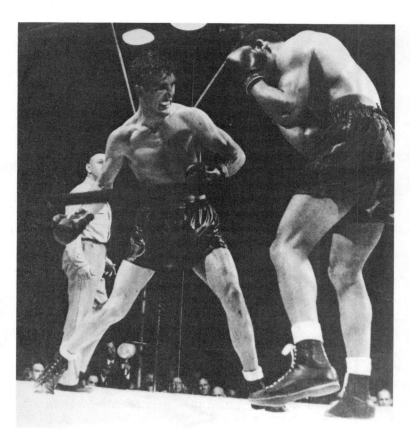

Billy Conn winding up to deliver a savage right to the head of the champ, Joe Louis, in the twelfth round of the famous Louis-Conn fight. *UPI photo*

Billy Conn delivering a left to Joe Louis' head in the tenth round of the famous Louis-Conn fight. *UPI photo*

Movie and boxing celebrities honoring Joe Louis on his sixtieth
birthday—left to right: Sugar Ray Robinson, Max Schmeling,
Joe Louis, Billy Conn, Gregory Peck, and Chuck Connors—Las
Vegas, Nevada, 1973. *UPI photo*

Billy Conn admiring Joe Louis' stripes, in the army, June 1942. *United States Signal Corps photo*

Billy Conn successfully defending his light-heavyweight title against Gus Lesnivich—note Conn's defense. *UPI photo*

Billy Conn at the end of the war in Europe, May 1945—Bob
Hope on his left and Jerry Colonna on his right. *United States
Signal Corps photo*

Billy Conn and the author at a banquet at which both men were honored, November 1981

Mary Louise and Billy Conn at Ocean City, New Jersey, mid-1941

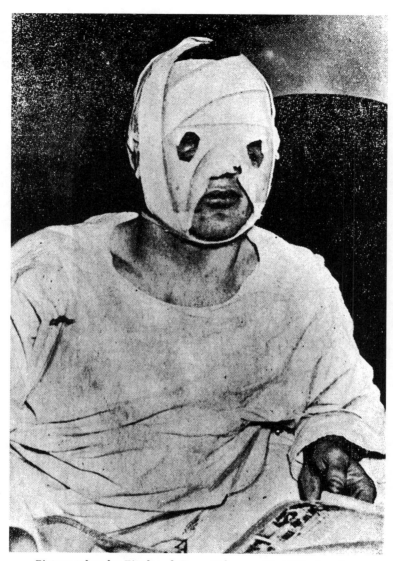

Picture taken by *Pittsburgh Press*, February 12, 1939, showing Billy Conn in Mercy Hospital after winning a bout with Fred Apostoli. The newspaper headlines read: "IF THIS IS THE WINNER, WHAT DOES THE LOSER LOOK LIKE?" The author dubbed this picture: "When Irish eyes are closing."

Mary Louise and Billy Conn at a reception, November 1981

Billy Conn and Joe Louis right after the fight of the century

Billy Conn speaking at a dinner at Bluefield, West Virginia, early in 1982

ROUND ELEVEN
The Kid Assesses the Champ

What can be said about a man who has been your hero for over four decades? There is really little to say that has not been said in the book; there are however, a few basic things that came into my mind as I was planning and preparing this book for publication.

First, many people have asked me just exactly what constitutes a hero in a young person's mind. First, I believe that the hero has to accomplish something and second, the hero has to do no wrong. I guess that pretty much tells the story about Billy.

I'll never forget the time I was irritated with a federal examiner because that man was a disruption to every member of our staff, and he seemed destined for me to take a crack at him. I was nevertheless quite upset that people could be so ignorant. Certainly the reader has been upset by a particular incident and has wanted revenge. Well, that is exactly how I happened to be a few years ago.

One night at the Champ's house, we were discussing what I was going to do to that examiner when he stepped foot into our bank. All of a sudden, the Champ took me by the arm and led me into the living room and said, "You idiot, I'm surprised at you. First of all, you're over thirty-five years old and people over thirty-five should not fight. Second, the business of banking is built on character, integrity, and trust. If you want to lose all of the things that you have built up over the years, then cream him; if you want to retain your high ideals, however, leave the ass alone."

Billy told me to feel sorry for the guy, for if he did not have my friendship, then he was definitely the loser. He suggested one other thing to me that showed his true character: the Champ said, "If you still feel this way about him, then get that man together with his boss and tell the boss in front of him what the problem happens to be because you should never talk behind a man's back. You should run right at him."

That evening the Champ, in effect, really scolded me and I didn't like it. I went into their large, beautiful living room and began to read a magazine. In about twenty minutes he came into the room and put his open hand down toward me and said, "Kid, let's shake. I think you know what I mean. Be the man that I know you are." Of course, I shook hands and that was the end of that episode.

As you can see, this marvelous man has integrity, character and, above all, class. I have never seen him raise his fists in anger or challenge anyone. It is amazing how many people come up to him and after a while they begin to tell the Champ how tough they happen to be and about their fighting experiences. The Champ smiles and always replies, "No kidding." When they leave he always tells me that everyone he ever talks to has won all their fights in and out of the ring. "It's funny," he said. "Even Joe Louis and I lost a few."

When I became twenty-one years of age, the Champ asked me if I knew the *Ten Commandments*. I told him that I did. To my surprise, he said, "Name them." Well, I struggled through six or seven of them and began to slow down. He immediately told me the remainder. He informed me that there were ten additional things he would like to pass on to me, for at age twenty-one I now had logic of reasoning and I should, by all means, listen to them.

I remember replying, "Go ahead, shoot. I'm ready to listen. I've listened to you for the past twelve years and you always gave me good advice."

Here are Conn's commandments:

1. Don't ever be a wise guy; they are not in demand.
2. It will be the obstacles in the world that will make you a better man.
3. Remember that the Lord told Solomon he would give him anything he so desired and Solomon chose wisdom.
4. Don't worry one bit when someone talks about you if what they say is not true; if one talks about you and what they say is, then you have a problem.
5. The worst thing in the world that can happen to you is nothing happening to you.
6. Be kind to all, friendly to many, and close to few.

7. Don't talk about people; doing so can't put money in your pocket.
8. You must always respect God, family, and country, and in that order.
9. Don't fight with anyone. If you win, really you have lost everything you have built during your lifetime.
10. Whatever your vocation may be, be the very best, and that comes through education and practice. Be a professional.

Several years later, I fondly renamed those things that the great Champ told me as the *Ten CONNmandments*. The above ten phrases are absolutely necessary for success, and I owe any success that I have to my hero and champion. Every parent and child should read those CONNmandments.

Billy Conn is a shy, loving man that I want the world to know about. When he fought totally unafraid the fight of the century, the 55 thousand people that saw him and the 20 million that heard the fight do not know the love and affection this man has for people. One night I heard him talking on the phone and some individual wanted twelve tickets to a professional football game. Billy replied, "Why, certainly."

He has helped more people than any man I have ever known, asking nothing in return. If you or your family are sick, he quietly goes to his bedroom with his rosaries. No one will ever know what he has done for me, for there just are no words to describe it.

One time while working on Guam as a civilian, I was watching two lightweights box on TV and a naval officer with enough scrambled eggs on his hat to make an omelet said that boxers today don't fight like Billy Conn used to fight. I told the naval officer that Billy Conn was my best friend, and he replied that Mickey Mouse was his best friend. Well, I just shut up. For one thing, I did know that Billy was my friend, and that wise guy would never have the opportunity of being Billy's friend. Billy is extremely well-known all over the world. I'm proud of him, and I believe he is indeed proud of me.

My wonderful mother and father have always said I was easy to raise, for if I started to give them a problem, they threatened to call the Champ. That always calmed me down; I wanted to do right so he would be proud of me. My mother always said that Billy was her son's "end of the rainbow."

I am so happy now that there are days we can be together since

I'm only 250 miles away and we either see each other once each week or communicate via telephone. Boy, am I a lucky guy, having the Champ as my best friend. No one can ever tell me there is no God, for God had to place Billy's hand on my head when I was eight years old. That changed the course of my life. The message is quite clear that I like the Champ.

When people do nice things for Billy, he really appreciates it. Often I hear him say that Bob Hope and Art Rooney are the two premium quarterbacks on the all-star team of nice guys. I think that's an excellent tribute from one man to another.

Shortly before my father died, he told me that Billy and I have a unique friendship. He said, "Please don't ever break that bond for it comes through your life only once." My father can rest in peace since nothing could ever detach the bond of love that I have for the Champ. In his quiet way, I know he is there should I need him and I know he feels that way about me. There is absolutely no way a young person can go astray if they have this kind of attachment to a person.

One of the great things of my life, down through the years, was to have Billy put me on. Let me explain what I mean by "putting one on." During my college days, I attended a small college in the southern part of Pennsylvania (Waynesburg College). I was only about one and a half hours from Pittsburgh, and sometimes in the evenings, I would go home to visit the Champ and my family—especially on the Saturdays when we did not have a football game. I had the habit of always trying to bring along a nice looking coed. I was very proud of the Champ, and I always tried to introduce him to my friends. Invariably, if the girl's name was Mary, everything would be pleasant all evening, and upon leaving his beautiful home, he would always say, "It has been great seeing you again. Keep in touch. And, by the way, it has been nice meeting you, RUTH!"

The girl would look at me, and once we got into the car, she would say, "Who in the hell is Ruth?"

Over and over I would plead my case that I did not know any Ruth, but, of course, to no avail. So one day, since the Champ always used the name Ruth, I decided to find a Ruth and take her up to visit with the Champ and his lovely wife, Mary Louise. Lo and behold, when we were leaving his home, he said, "It was great seeing you again. Keep in touch. And, by the way, it has been nice meeting you, MARY!" Of course, you know the rest of the story.

61

But on this particular night, I turned around and said, "One of these days, you are going to get the greatest left-hook you ever got."

Billy turned around, laughed, and said, "Listen kid, you know where I live!" He shook my hand and walked off.

In early 1982, I had the privilege of becoming the international president of the National Association of Review Appraisers, which is located in St. Paul, Minnesota. This organization is one of the finest and most honorable groups I have ever met, and I was quite proud to become the international president. This position took me to the far corners of the United States, as well as the world, attending meetings and making numerous speeches. Since the Champ knows important people in all areas of the country, as well as the world, he would tell me, "When you get to your destination, by all means, look up several of my dear friends and give them my personal regards." I would get the names and look them up. To my amazement, they were all dead. The first few times, I would come back and tell the Champ that all of his friends on the list of names had passed away.

He would look at me and say, "Is that a fact?" Every time I went away he'd pull the same thing on me. This was his way of just "putting me on."

Now when I go away, I continue to ask him to give me names of his friends, and he continues to give me names. When I return, I always say, "So and so said to tell you hello."

And he looks at me and says, "He is a swell guy." To this day, he will never admit that he knows these people are dead. I really enjoy his blend of humor because, let me tell you, if he does not like you, he will give you the coldest brush off in the world—so cold, you would think you were under ten tons of ice. We seem to know just exactly how far to go with each other, and I really think this is the mark of true friendship.

In June of 1982, I experienced one of the happiest moments of my life. After all the years of help that Billy had given to me, including his personal advice and always his encouragement, he now asked me for advice. He was perplexed about a very large apartment building that he owned, and he wanted my advice on whether to keep the building or sell it. He said he would do whatever I thought was best. Here, for the first time in my life, I had a chance to give this great and good man my personal, undivided advice. After weeks and weeks of reviewing the project, I finally advised the Champ to sell and to invest his money in insured investments for dear Mary Louise's benefit and his security. Without question, I was telling the Champ what I would personally do.

He looked at me and said, "Let's do it." And that was that! As this book goes to press, he still continues to thank me. I always reply that I had to make the best decision for him because he has the greatest left-hook in the business, and I do not want to be on the other end of it.

In early January, 1982, I had the pleasure of attending a Rotary Club in southern West Virginia. I showed the great Louis-Conn Fight film. At the end of the exciting film, the president of the club asked the members if they had any questions they would like to ask me regarding Billy Conn. One gentleman seated in the audience, said to me, "You really love Billy Conn."

"Of course," I replied, "and I am glad you can see that."

The gentleman then asked, "What do you consider his greatest attribute?"

I thought for a moment and said, "I cannot give you one thing, but I could probably give you three or four outstanding features about him." I said, "First of all, he does not talk about anyone, and he is the bravest man I have ever met." Then I described some of my reasons for saying he was brave. First and foremost, prior to the Louis-Conn fight, Billy's heartbeat was 15 percent less than the average heartbeat. The normal heart beats about 70 beats per minute; his heartbeat was about 59 beats per minute. Secondly, he fell asleep prior to the fight. This certainly proves that he was totally unafraid. He always told me that no man is afraid if he knows his business, and without question, he knows his business. I will never forget how Billy would sit in the corner of the ring between rounds. He would sit very erect, staring straight across the ring at the other fighter. He exuded great confidence, and you always felt that he was totally in command. He never slouched in the corner while his handlers were working on him. He sat straight as a soldier.

I remember one time he was matched with one of the greatest middleweights of all times, Oscar Rankins. I reviewed Rankins' record and found that in all of his fights he either knocked out his opponent or knocked him down. I mentioned this to Billy, prior to the fight, and he said, "I don't bother to look up any records. I will try hard and I will win—and I will try not to get hit."

I said, "Champ, this man can really hit."

63

Well, we found out in the eighth round. Rankins connected with a shot to Billy's head and it floored Billy. This was the second time he had been floored in his career, and at that time, he had had forty-eight professional fights. After the fight, he looked at me and said, "Oscar Rankins can hit!" Billy was floored for eight counts in that eighth round, but he came back to win the fight.

Then I informed this fine member of the Rotary Club that another attribute of Billy's was the fact that he has never lied to me. In fact, as far as I know, he has never lied to anyone. He has always been a God-loving individual. I concluded by saying that Billy Conn has his head squarely on his shoulders. When my father passed away, he said to me, "We have lost a great friend, but I want you to remember, death is the fairest thing in all the world, because it happens to everyone."

As I was driving home after the Rotary meeting, I thought about something to add about my dear friend Billy Conn. I would like to add this information for the readers of this book. Billy told me one day when I was a young working man to make every effort to seek a boss who was quiet, had strong convictions, and was reasonably bright. "And above all," he said, "remember, very few people get ahead when they work for a big mouth." He informed me that in 1862, Abraham Lincoln, speaking to a group of people, said that the reason a man has two ears and one mouth is because he should listen twice as much as he talks. I sought employment with people who had these virtues, and some of the best training I ever had in my life was from this caliber of men. I can think of two men that had a profound impact on my life. One was my dear friend Robert C. Downie, who was president of the Pittsburgh National Bank. Bob was a lawyer and one of the youngest army colonels in the history of the Army, during World War II, and, I believe, the greatest bank president of a major bank in the United States. This man taught me a great deal about the professional world of banking. Then in the early 1970s, I had the pleasure of working for the United States Government and the privilege of working for the Director of Territorial Affairs, a man by the name of Fred M. Zeder II. Fred has since gone on to become ambassador of the Pacific, a position for which he was nominated by a great American, Vice-President George Bush. I should have told the Club that the way I feel about Billy Conn, there was no way I could say he was great in just one way.

Many people have asked me why Billy Conn was so great as

a professional fighter. I imagine this question has been asked literally hundreds of times. I feel that since I have known the Champ for all these years, I can best answer their questions in this manner.

First and foremost, Billy Conn was taught by the best fight manager in the world, Johnny Ray. It has often been said that Johnny Ray could teach you more in ninety days than the average manager could teach his pupil in a lifetime. In addition, Billy Conn had great stamina and kept himself in superb physical condition. He possessed a strong desire to win. I might also add that Billy had tremendous peripheral vision. He was extrememly fast—in fact I have seen him hit a man two or three jabs with both of his feet off the canvas at the same time. You cannot say that about any other boxer in the world. Last, but by far, not the least, Billy had a great defense. He had the ability to always keep his hands held high to avoid being hit.

The question drifts back to me about what happened to Billy Conn the night he fought Joe Louis. This again is very simple. Billy did everything right through the twelfth round. The last thirty seconds that Billy was on his feet in the thirteenth round he literally did everything wrong. First, he was warned by Johnny Ray not to try to slug it out with the great Joe Louis. Billy, of course, replied that he was going for a knockout. Billy Conn did not possess the power of Joe Louis because he was thirty pounds lighter. When Billy Conn went on the attack in the last thirty seconds of the fight, he opened himself for Louis to move in. In other words, Billy threw his guard to the caution of the wind, and Louis, with his tremendous punch-power, was able to penetrate Billy's guard and, therefore, with five or six very stiff blows, he was able to defeat the great Billy Conn.

The last thing I would like to say about this great man's ability in the ring is that Billy, as light as he was, had the ability to take a punch; therefore, he had all that was necessary—vision, stamina, defense, and the ability to absorb punishment. There will never be another fighter quite like Billy Conn.

One thing I learned from Billy Conn was to make every attempt to be an achiever. According to Billy Conn, the only way you can be an achiever is to work with achievers, associate with achievers, and compete with achievers. All of my working life, I have tried to do this. As I write this book, I look back on some of the happenings in southern West Virginia. Every one of my staff members is an achiever, the people I associate with are definitely achievers, and the executive officers of the other banks are achievers. So again,

Billy has to be right. His marvelous ability came at an early age when he boxed with champions who came down to train. He entered the ring and trained with them. These men were achievers. His manager, Johnny Ray, was an achiever. Billy, during his career, fought and beat twenty world champions, and they were all achievers. Therefore, young men and women must surround themselves with achievers.

ROUND TWELVE
The Boxer and
the Banker Today

The Champ is well entrenched in his beautiful home in Pittsburgh with basically not a care in the world. He is close by his two oldest boys, while his youngest son, Michael, is in Alexandria, Virginia, and his lovely daughter resides in the Chicago area. Incidentally, after his beloved Pittsburgh, the Champ loves Chicago and San Francisco. He has told me many times these two cities are the only other places he would ever live.

I am located 250 miles due south of Pittsburgh in the Bluefield area of West Virginia, where I am president of a $30 million bank. The Champ and I have long learned never to be out of communication with each other more than one week and we have kept our word on this.

Many individuals have asked me what the attraction is that makes our great friendship unique. My late father always told me that you are only a millionaire if you have a friend that through it all is with you. Well, then, I am a millionaire for Billy has been beside me in good times as well as bad. He has never lied to me, and he has taught me the values of life that are necessary to get through this world and for that I thank him so very much.

When I'm in Pittsburgh, the Conn residence is my hangout. I usually arrive there about 4:30 P.M. on a Saturday afternoon and, during the winter months, we go down to the great restaurants in the neighborhood, usually getting our favorite dish—lobster tail. In the summer, we sit on his beautiful back porch and grill steaks. Billy can grill pretty well by the watchful eye of beautiful Mary Louise. Generally, we watch TV until 11:30 P.M. Sunday, I depart for good old West Virginia. I always call him when I get home to inform him of my safe arrival.

This book would certainly not be complete without acknowledging that beautiful girl Mary Louise. She is the greatest. Loaded with personality, warmth and charm, she is simply outstanding. I always ask her how she is doing and it's always the same, "wonderful." The four kids, Tim, Billy, Michael and Suzanne, are great and without the genuine help of Tim and Michael the book could not have been written. To know that you can talk to or see your best friends every week is worth more than anything in this world and, as we move forward with Father Time, it's great to be with people you love.

Well, Champ, there you have it. Thanks to those marvelous kids and the beautiful Mary Louise, I have recorded as accurately as possible your great life as well as the impact you have made on this kid.

You know, Champ, I'll never forget the time when I got excited about the possibilities of not getting the charter for the bank I started in 1962, and your words to me were as follows: "Don't get excited for when you lose your head your ass goes with it." It's the greatest one-liner I ever heard, but then you were always the master of those one-liners.

I have always told my friends that all in me that is good I owe to you and anything bad I accept the blame completely. Well, enough of my ramblings. You were never one to go on and on about anything so I guess I'll close.

I'll be in Pittsburgh this Saturday and, if my memory is correct, it is my turn to buy the lobster tails. Tell Mary Louise I'll be at your home between 4:30 and 5:00 P.M. and I would like to stay in the Jack Dempsey room. After all these years I have really gotten used to that great room. See you then, Champ. Oh, by the way, there is a great fight on TV Saturday—two southpaws. I bet you pick the wrong fighter again.

For many years, I have never signed off without saying my true feelings about you so, until I see you Saturday, I just want you and the world to know that you are some kind of a guy.

Love and best wishes to the family.

P.S. I never told you, Champ, but in 1960 several men asked my dad to describe Billy Conn to them in one sentence. After thinking for a minute, my father replied, "Billy Conn is a certified professional—inside and outside of the ring." You know, Champ, that really tells it all.

APPENDIX
INTERESTING FACTS AND DATES

1. Conn fought and beat twenty former world champs.
2. Conn fought ten times in Madison Square Garden and won every fight.
3. Conn received five boxing awards including the Hall of Fame Award in 1965.
4. His record includes seventy-five fights—forty-nine won by decision and fourteen by knockout. He had one draw, lost nine bouts and was knocked out twice.
5. On April 4, 1941, Billy Conn knocked out Gunnar Barlund in eight rounds. Barlund was rated thirteenth among the heavyweights in 1936. In 1937, Bob Pastor was rated eighth in the heavyweight division. Conn knocked out Pastor in the thirteenth round on September 6, 1940.
6. Conn's toughest fights in ascending order have been the second Apostoli fight, second Kreiger fight, Oscar Rankins, and Joe Louis. Billy Conn had abnormally easy wins over heavyweights due to his speed and fighting ability.
7. There were five world champions from Pittsburgh during Billy Conn's professional career: Teddy Yarosz, middleweight, won the title on September 11, 1934; Fritzie Zivic, welterweight, won the title on October 4, 1940; Jackie Wilson, featherweight, won the title on November 18, 1941; Sammy Angott, lightweight, won the title on December 19, 1941; and Billy Soose, middleweight, won the title on May 9, 1941. Billy Conn won the light-heavyweight title on July 13, 1939.
8. There are nine world boxing champions from the Pittsburgh area from 1924 to 1939. In addition to the above they are (1.) Harry Greb, Middleweight and Light-Heavyweight Champion, the only man ever to defeat Gene Tunney (May 23, 1922, New York). Harry Greb defeated Gene Tunney for the vacant light-heavy-

weight title. (2.) George Chip, Middleweight Champion, October 11, 1913. Knocked out Frank Klaus in the sixth round on December 23, 1913. (3.) Frank Klaus, Middleweight Champion, March 5, 1913.

9. From 1936 to 1939, Billy Conn fought and beat twenty former world champs. Billy won the light-heavyweight crown on July 13, 1939, by defeating Melio Bettina in fifteen rounds. Billy gave Bettina a quick chance to regain the crown by fighting him again on September 25, 1939, in Pittsburgh. Conn won the match by decision in fifteen rounds. Many of Billy's friends, including the author, objected to Billy agreeing to a rematch within ten weeks after winning the title, but Billy replied, "Don't worry, he won't get it back."

10. There are twelve chapters in this book to symbolize that for twelve rounds Billy Conn was indeed the Heavyweight Champion of the world.

11. Honors Billy Conn has received include the Edward J. Neil Memorial Award, 1939; Fighter-of-the-Year Award, 1940; Boxing Hall of Fame, 1965; Athlete of the Twentieth Century, 1981; and, Rocky Marciano Award, 1981.

12. Billy Conn was knocked down twice. The first time was May 27, 1937, in Pittsburgh at the hands of Oscar Rankins. Billy got up at the count of eight and went on to win the fight, in the ten-round battle. He was knocked down again September 14, 1938, at the hands of Ray Actis. This was in the sixth round. He came back to K.O. Actis in the eighth round. The only other knockdowns were two knockouts by Joe Louis.

NOTES ON JOE LOUIS

1. Joe Louis fought seventy fights, thirteen won by decision, and fifty-three by knockout, one lost by decision, and one on a foul, and was knocked out two times.

2. Joe Louis defeated Charlie Massare, a Pittsburgh fighter, on November 30, 1934. In 1933, Charlie Massare was rated eighth in the heavyweight division. When Louis defeated Massare it jumped Joe Louis, who was not in the top-ten heavyweights in 1933, to ninth place in 1934.

MARGARITE "MAGGIE" McFARLAND CONN

Billy's mother was born in County Cork, Ireland. She came to this country with her family at the age of eighteen. She spoke with a pronounced brogue, was a traditional, devout Catholic, and physically a large heavy-set woman. She was later to become the force, the inspiration and the shaper of many of Billy's qualities—in and outside the ring—determination, the ability to bear pain and suffer quietly and courage beyond what most individuals experience.

Maggie had a special relationship with Billy. In fact, the name "Maggie" was a special name Billy called his mom, and no one else. When Maggie realized Billy wanted to be a professional boxer and not follow his father into steamfitting, she encouraged him completely and unequivocally. She was proud of Billy before he achieved fame, felt he was a good boy, and imbued in him the desire to do the "right" thing.

Maggie was a jovial, outgoing, warm and friendly person. She was the peacemaker in the family. She had an intuitive sense as to how far to let the boys and, sometimes dad and the boys, fight. When Maggie said "break," the fighting stopped. She was deeply religious—one who could accept God's will. She was wise beyond her limited education.

She was simple, loving, proud, and, as the Almighty was to discover, an enduring woman. Maggie became ill in her late thirties with cancer. She bore this cross quietly, with no patience for pity or sympathy. In her last year, while bedridden, Billy used to slip up to her bedroom with her favorite drink, champagne, against doctor's orders, and the two would slowly get smashed—easing the pain and burden Maggie carried.

Shortly before the Louis fight, Billy went upstairs to see Maggie and presented her with a diamond bracelet.

He said, "Maggie, this is for you. The next time I see you, I'll be heavyweight champ of the world."

Maggie responded, "Billy, the bracelet is beautiful but give it to Mary Louise. Her father, Jimmy, will come around. Don't let him hold you back. And, son, the next time I see you . . . will be in Paradise."

Maggie died one week after the Louis fight. Billy never saw her again, but he followed his heart and her wishes and married Mary

Louise one day after the funeral because that is what Maggie would have wanted.

MARIE RICE McCONNELL

The author's mother was born in Carnegie, Pennsylvania (western Pennsylvania), one of three daughters of Philip and Katherine Rice. Marie attended McKeesport High School, McKeesport, Pennsylvania, but later graduated from a business school as a secretary. She worked for forty years for the Pan-American Life Insurance Company in Pittsburgh, Pennsylvania, as a secretary to the state agent.

I was an only child and extremely close to my mother. My mother was a beautiful redhead, intelligent, quiet, and witty. She had to work primarily because our family was caught up in the Depression.

While in her early fifties she came down with severe heart failure; she continued her battle with great and quiet courage. One of her brightest moments in life was the outstanding friendship that developed between Billy Conn and me. My mother passed away in 1968 knowing that she had performed outstanding service to her community, country, and family.

RATING TABLES

Note: The following tables are reprinted through the courtesy of *Ring Magazine*.

RING RATINGS
1 9 3 7

Heavyweights
World Champion
Joe Louis
1. Max Schmeling
2. Tommy Farr
3. Nathan Mann
4. Alberto Lovell
5. Tony Galento
6. Jimmy Adamick
7. Lou Nova
8. Bob Pastor
9. Roscoe Toles
10. Andre Lenglet

Light Heavyweights
World Champion
John Henry Lewis
1. Al Gainer
2. Tiger Jack Fox
3. Jock McAvoy
4. Eddie Wenstob
5. Ray Actis
6. Ralph De John
7. Billy Conn
8. Gus Lesnevich
9. Melio Bettina
10. Fred Lenhart

Middleweights
World Champion
Freddie Steele
1. Fred Apostoli
2. Al Hostak
3. Carmelo Candel
4. George Black
5. Young Corbett
6. Ben Brown
7. Glen Lee
8. Teddy Yarosz
9. Lou Brouillard
10. Ken Overlin

Welterweights
World Champion
Barney Ross
1. Ceferino Garcia
2. Jack Carroll
3. Gustave Eder
4. Saverio Turiello
5. Izzy Jannazzo
6. Holman Williams
7. Cocoa Kid
8. Jimmy Leto
9. Fritzie Zivic
10. Ralph Zannelli

Lightweights
World Champion
Lou Ambers
1. Pedro Montanez
2. Davey Day
3. Wesley Ramey
4. Billy Beauhuld
5. Eddie Cool
6. Johnny Bellus
7. Paul Junior
8. Petey Sarron
9. Frankie Wallace
10. Eddie McGeever

Featherweights
World Champion
Henry Armstrong
1. Freddie Miller
2. Leo Rodak
3. Young Rightmire
4. Jackie Wilson
5. Tony Chavez
6. Ginger Foran
7. Benny Sharkey
8. Kid Chocolate
9. Joey Archibald
10. Johnny Cusick

Bantamweights
World Champion
Harry Jeffra
1. K. O. Morgan
2. Sixto Escobar
3. Lou Salica
4. Indian Quintana
5. Georgie Pace
6. Spider Armstrong
7. Baby Yack
8. Johnny King
9. Tobe De La Rosa
10. Aurel Toma

Flyweights
World Champion
Benny Lynch
1. Peter Kane
2. Pierre Louis
3. Tiny Bostock
4. Small Montana
5. Jackie Jurich
6. Jim Warnock
7. Valentin Anglemann
8. Joe Curran
9. Tut Whalley
10. Frank Kid Bonser

RING RATINGS
1 9 3 8

Heavyweights
World Champion
Joe Louis
1. Lou Nova
2. Max Baer
3. Bob Pastor
4. Tony Galento
5. Maxie Rosenbloom
6. Len Harvey
7. Red Burman
8. Roscoe Toles
9. Gus Dorazio
10. Tommy Farr

Light Heavyweights
World Champion
John Henry Lewis
1. Tiger Jack Fox
2. Melio Bettina
3. Ron Richards
4. Gus Lesnevich
5. Len Harvey
6. Adolph Heuser
7. Jock McAvoy
8. Al Gainer
9. Billy Conn
10. Ambrose Palmer

Middleweights
Title Vacant

1. Fred Apostoli
2. Solly Krieger
3. Ron Richards
4. Ken Overlin
5. Teddy Yarosz
6. Walter Woods
7. Ben Brown
8. Al Hostak
9. Jock McAvoy
10. Ginger Sadd

Welterweights
World Champion
Henry Armstrong
1. Ceferino Garcia
2. Fritzie Zivic
3. Charley Burley
4. Ernie Roderick
5. Steve Mamakos
6. Saverio Turiello
7. Sammy Luftspring
8. Jake Kilrain
9. Kid Frattini
10. Jimmy Leto

Lightweights
World Champion
Henry Armstrong
1. Lou Ambers
2. Pedro Montanez
3. Davey Day
4. Baby Arizmendi
5. Sammy Angott
6. Billy Beauhuld
7. Aldo Spoldi
8. Petey Sarron
9. Maxie Berger
10. Tommy Cross

Featherweights
Title Vacant

1. Leo Rodak
2. Pete Scalzo
3. Dave Castilloux
4. Joey Archibald
5. Mike Belloise
6. Chalky Wright
7. Johnny Hutchinson
8. Al Reid
9. Freddie Miller
10. Claude Varner

Bantamweights
World Champion
Sixto Escobar
1. K. O. Morgan
2. Lou Salica
3. Georgie Pace
4. Kid Tanner
5. Aurel Toma
6. Henry Hook
7. Pancho Villa
8. Johnny Gaudes
9. Teddy O'Neil
10. Spider Kelly

Flyweights
World Champion
Peter Kane
1. Little Dado
2. Small Montana
3. Kid Tanner
4. Tut Whalley
5. Jackie Jurich
6. Dennis Cahill
7. Carlo Urbinati
8. Tiny Bostock
9. Paddy Ryan
10. Tommy Farriker

RING RATINGS
1 9 3 9

Heavyweights
World Champion
Joe Louis
1. Tony Galento
2. Bob Pastor
3. Lou Nova
4. Tommy Farr
5. Max Schmeling
6. Johnny Paychek
7. Red Burman
8. Gunnar Barlund
9. Roscoe Toles
10. Lee Savold

Light Heavyweights
World Champion
Billy Conn
1. Gus Lesnevich
2. Melio Bettina
3. Len Harvey
4. Jock McAvoy
5. Dave Clark
6. Tiger Jack Fox
7. Teddy Yarosz
8. Al Gainer
9. Larry Lane
10. Lee Oma

Middleweights
Title Vacant

1. Ceferino Garcia
2. Al Hostak
3. Ken Overlin
4. Ron Richards
5. Ben Brown
6. Lloyd Marshall
7. Ossie Stewart
8. Victor Dellicurti
9. Nate Bolden
10. Tony Zale

Welterweights
World Champion
Henry Armstrong
1. Fritzie Zivic
2. Holman Williams
3. Milt Aron
4. Ernie Roderick
5. Charley Burley
6. Mike Kaplan
7. Cocoa Kid
8. Maxie Berger
9. Jimmy Leto
10. Steve Mamakos

Lightweights
World Champion
Lou Ambers
1. Davey Day
2. Sammy Angott
3. Eric Boon
4. Wesley Ramey
5. Jackie Wilson
6. Bob Montgomery
7. Pete Lello
8. George Crouch
9. Leo Rodak
10. Billy Maher

Featherweights
World Champion
Joey Archibald
1. Al Mancini
2. Simon Chavez
3. Pete Scalzo
4. Jackie Wilson
5. Harry Jeffra
6. Chalky Wright
7. Jimmy Perrin
8. Frankie Covelli
9. Richard Lemos
10. Bobby Green

Bantamweights
Title Vacant

1. K. O. Morgan
2. Georgie Pace
3. Lou Salica
4. Peter Kane
5. Tony Olivera
6. Little Pancho
7. Kui Kong Young
8. Jim Brady
9. Benny Goldberg
10. Tommy Kiene

Flyweights
Title Vacant

1. Little Dado
2. Enrico Urbinati
3. Jackie Paterson
4. Joe Curran
5. Tiny Bostock
6. Small Montana
7. Jackie Jurich
8. Raoul Degryse
9. Paddy Ryan
10. Rinty Monaghan

R I N G   R A T I N G S
1 9 4 0

Heavyweights
World Champion
Joe Louis
1. Max Baer
2. Arturo Godoy
3. Red Burman
4. Abe Simon
5. Buddy Walker
6. Buddy Baer
7. Pat Comiskey
8. Lee Savold
9. Otis Thomas
10. Lem Franklin

Light Heavyweights
World Champion
Billy Conn
1. Jimmy Webb
2. Anton Christoforidis
3. Melio Bettina
4. Gus Lesnevich
5. Teddy Yarosz
6. Turkey Thompson
7. Tommy Tucker
8. Jimmy Reeves
9. Solly Krieger
10. Lloyd Marshall

Middleweights
Title Vacant

1. Ken Overlin
2. Tony Zale
3. Billy Soose
4. Archie Moore
5. Steve Belloise
6. Jimmy Bivins
7. Al Hostak
8. Georgie Abrams
9. Tami Mauriello
10. Ernie Vigh

Welterweights
World Champion
Fritzie Zivic
1. Henry Armstrong
2. Izzy Jannazzo
3. Charley Burley
4. Jimmy Leto
5. Mike Kaplan
6. Maxie Berger
7. Holman Williams
8. Cocoa Kid
9. Tony Marteliano
10. Baby Breese

Lightweights
World Champion
Lew Jenkins
1. Sammy Angott
2. Jackie Wilson
3. Pete Lello
4. Tommy Speigal
5. Dave Castilloux
6. Bob Montgomery
7. Toby Vigil
8. Baby Arizmendi
9. Aldo Spoldi
10. Yucatan Kid

Featherweights
World Champion
Harry Jeffra
1. Bill Speary
2. Chalky Wright
3. Pete Scalzo
4. Joe Marinelli
5. Jimmy Perin
6. Larry Bolvin
7. Bobby Ivy
8. Young Rightmire
9. Vincenzo Dell Orto
10. Al Mancini

Bantamweights
Title Vacant

1. Tommy Forte
2. Tony Olivera
3. Lou Salica
4. Rush Dalma
5. Kui Kong Young
6. Jim Brady
7. Kid Tanner
8. Chick Delaney
9. Freddie Pope
10. Johnny Juliano

Flyweights
Title Vacant

1. Jackie Paterson
2. Little Pancho
3. Little Dado
4. Manuel Oritz
5. Jackie Jurich
6. Paddy Ryan
7. Tiny Bostock
8. Joe Curran
9. Jimmy Stewart
10. Small Montana

RING RATINGS
1941

Heavyweights
World Champion
Joe Louis
1. Billy Conn
2. Lem Franklin
3. Bob Pastor
4. Melio Bettina
5. Abe Simon
6. Turkey Thompson
7. Buddy Baer
8. Lou Nova
9. Arturo Godoy
10. Roscoe Toles

Light Heavyweights
World Champion
Gus Lesnevich
1. Booker Beckwith
2. Ken Overlin
3. Jimmy Bivins
4. Mose Brown
5. Billy Soose
6. Anton Christoforidis
7. Tommy Tucker
8. Joey Maxim
9. Erv Sarlen
10. Lloyd Marshall

Middleweights
World Champion
Tony Zale
1. Georgie Abrams
2. Ezzard Charles
3. Ernie Vigh
4. Coley Welch
5. Ceferino Garcia
6. Steve Belloise
7. Antonio Fernandez
8. Fred Apostoli
9. Ron Richards
10. Ossie Stewart

Welterweights
World Champion
Freddie Cochrane
1. Ray Robinson
2. Jackie Wilson
3. Fritzie Zivic
4. Young Kid McCoy
5. Charley Burley
6. Holman Williams
7. Cocoa Kid
8. Izzy Jannazzo
9. Ron Richards
10. Norman Rubio

Lightweights
World Champion
Sammy Angott
1. Bob Montgomery
2. Lenny Mancini
3. Dave Castilloux
4. Ray Lunny
5. Juan Zurita
6. George Latka
7. Chester Rico
8. Bobby Ruffin
9. Harry Hurst
10. Lew Jenkins

Featherweights
World Champion
Chalky Wright
1. Jackie Wilson
2. Richie Lemos
3. Pedro Hernandez
4. Harry Jeffra
5. Sal Bartolo
6. Bobby Ivy
7. Mike Raffa
8. Jimmy Hatcher
9. Charley Costantino
10. Bill Speary

Bantamweights
World Champion
Lou Salica
1. Kui Kong Young
2. Manuel Ortiz
3. Rush Dalma
4. Jim Brady
5. Horace Mann
6. Tony Olivera
7. Tommy Forte
8. Kenny Lindsay
9. Peter Kane
10. Jimmy Stubbs

Flyweights
Title Vacant

1. Jackie Paterson
2. Little Dado
3. Joe Curran
4. Luis Castillo
5. Paddy Ryan
6. Johnny Shaughnessy
7. Tiny Bostock
8. Small Montana
9. Lupe Cordoza
10. Humberto Espinosa

79

RING RATINGS
1 9 4 5

Heavyweights
World Champion
Joe Louis
1. Billy Conn
2. Tami Mauriello
3. Jimmy Bivins
4. Elmer Ray
5. Bruce Woodcock
6. Lee Oma
7. Freddie Schott
8. Arturo Godoy
9. Jersey Joe Walcott
10. Joe Baksi

Light Heavyweights
World Champion
Gus Lesnevich
1. Archie Moore
2. Phil Muscato
3. Billy Grant
4. Lloyd Marshall
5. Joe Kahut
6. Nate Bolden
7. Jack Johnson
8. Freddie Mills
9. Billy Smith
10. Fitzie Fitzpatrick

Middleweights
World Champion
Tony Zale
1. Holman Williams
2. Charley Burley
3. Jake LaMotta
4. Rocky Graziano
5. Marcel Cerdan
6. Bee Bee Washington
7. Aaron Wade
8. Wildcat George Henry
9. Jimmy Edgar
10. Bert Lytell

Welterweights
World Champion
Freddie Cochrane

1. Ray Robinson
2. Jimmy Doyle
3. Tippy Larkin
4. Freddie Archer
5. Nick Moran
6. Arthur Danabar
7. Johnny Greco
8. Sammy Angott
9. Tony Janiro
10. Chuck Hunter

Lightweights
Title Vacant

1. Allie Stolz
2. Dave Castilloux
3. Willie Joyce
4. Ike Williams
5. Bob Montgomery
6. Bobby Ruffin
7. Ronnie James
8. Freddie Dawson
9. Bobby Yaeger
10. Enrique Bolanos

Featherweights
World Champion
Willie Pep
1. Sal Bartolo
2. Chalky Wright
3. Phil Terranova
4. Carlos Chavez
5. Kid Zefine
6. Al Phillips
7. Freddie Russo
8. Jackie Graves
9. Jimmy Stubbs
10. Charley Riley

Bantamweights
World Champion
Manuel Ortiz
1. Benny Goldberg
2. Tony Olivera
3. Luis Catillo
4. Simon Vergera
5. Sammy Reynolds
6. Norman Lewis
7. Gus Foran
8. Ronnie Clayton
9. Young Giant
10. Cliff Anderson

Flyweights
World Champion
Jackie Paterson

1. Seaman Terry Allen
2. Bunty Doran
3. Joe Curran
4. Rinty Monaghan
5. Luis Galvani
6. Alec Murphy
7. Hugh Cameron
8. Tommy Burney
9. George Parkes
10. Billy Clinton

BILLY CONN'S RECORD

Note: Conn began boxing professionally in 1935. By 1937 he was listed seventh in the light-heavyweight division.

BILLY CONN
(William David Conn, Jr.)
(The Pittsburgh Kid)
Born, October 8, 1917, East Liberty, Pa. Weight,
142-187 lbs. Height, 6 ft. Managed by Johnny Ray.

1935

	—Dick Woodwer, Fairmont	L	4
	—John Lewis, Charleston	KO	3
	—Paddy Gray, Pittsburgh	W	4
	—Bob Dorman, Clarksburg	W	6
Feb.	25—Ray Eberle, Pittsburgh	L	6
	—Johnny Birek, Pittsburgh	W	6
	—Stan Nagey, Wheeling	W	4
Apr.	8—George Schley, Pittsburgh	KO	6
Apr.	25—Ralph Gizzy, Pittsburgh	L	4
June	3—Ray Eberle, Pittsburgh	W	6
June	10—Ralph Gizzy, Pittsburgh	L	6
July	9—Teddy Movan, Pittsburgh	L	6
July	29—Ray Eberle, Pittsburgh	W	4
Aug.	19—Teddy Movan, Pittsburgh	L	4
Sept.	9—Georgie Leggins, Pittsburgh	W	4
Oct.	7—Johnny Yurcini, Johnson	W	6
Oct.	14—Teddy Movan, Pittsburgh	D	6
Nov.	18—Steve Walters, Pittsburgh	W	6

1936

Jan.	—Johnny Yurcini, Washington, Pa.	W	6
Jan.	27—Johnny Yurcini, Pittsburgh	KO	4
Feb.	3—Louis (Kid) Cook, Pittsburgh	W	6
Feb.	17—Louis (Kid) Cook, Pittsburgh	W	8
Mar.	16—Steve Nickleash, Pittsburgh	W	6
Apr.	13—Steve Nickleash, Pittsburgh	W	6
Apr.	27—General Burrows, Pittsburgh	W	6
May	19—Dick Ambrose, Pittsburgh	W	6
May	27—Honeyboy Jones, Pittsburgh	W	8
June	3—Honeyboy Jones, Pittsburgh	W	10
June	15—General Burrows, Pittsburgh	W	8
July	30—Teddy Movan, Pittsburgh	W	8
Aug.	10—Teddy Movan, Pittsburgh	W	8
Sept.	8—Honeyboy Jones, Pittsburgh	W	10
Sept.	21—Roscoe Manning, Pittsburgh	KO	5
Oct.	19—Charlie Weise, Pittsburgh	W	10
Oct.	22—Ralph Chong, Pittsburgh	W	10
Dec.	2—Jimmy Brown, Pittsburgh	KO	9
Dec.	28—Fritzie Zivic, Pittsburgh	W	10

1937

Mar.	11—Babe Risko, Pittsburgh	W	10
May	3—Vince Dundee, Pittsburgh	W	10
May	27—Oscar Rankins, Pittsburgh	W	10
June	30—Teddy Yarosz, Pittsburgh	W	12
Aug.	13—Young Corbett III, San Francisco	L	10
Sept.	30—Teddy Yarosz, Pittsburgh	W	15
Nov.	8—Young Corbett III, Pittsburgh	W	10
Dec.	16—Solly Krieger, Pittsburgh	L	12

1938

Jan.	24—Honeyboy Jones, Pittsburgh	W	12
Apr.	4—Domenic Ceccarelli, Pittsburgh	W	10
May	10—Eric Seelig, Pittsburgh	W	10
July	25—Teddy Yarosz, Pittsburgh	L	12
Sept.	14—Ray Actis, San Francisco	KO	8
Oct.	27—Honeyboy Jones, Pittsburgh	W	10
Nov.	28—Solly Krieger, Pittsburgh	W	12

1939

Jan.	6—Fred Apostoli, New York	W	10
Feb.	10—Fred Apostoli, New York	W	15
May	12—Solly Krieger, New York	W	12
July	13—Melio Bettina, New York	W	15
	(Won Vacant World Light Heavyweight Title)		
Aug.	14—Gus Dorazio, Philadelphia	KO	8
Sept.	25—Melio Bettina, Pittsburgh	W	15
	(Retained World Light Heavyweight Title)		
Nov.	17—Gus Lesnevich, New York	W	15
	(Retained World Light Heavyweight Title)		

1940

Jan.	10—Henry Cooper, New York	W	12
June	5—Gus Lesnevich, Detroit	W	15
	(Retained World Light Heavyweight Title)		
Sept.	6—Bob Pastor, New York	KO	13
Oct.	18—Al McCoy, Boston	W	10
Nov.	29—Lee Savold, New York	W	12

1941

Feb.	27—Ira Hughes, Clarksburg	KO	4
Mar.	6—Dan Hassett, Washington, D.C. ...	KO	5
Apr.	4—Gunnar Barlund, Chicago	KO	8
May	—Relinquished world light heavyweight title.		
May	26—Buddy Knox, Pittsburgh	KO	8
June	18—Joe Louis, New York	KO by	13
	(For World Heavyweight Title)		

1942

Jan.	12—Henry Cooper, Toledo	W	12
Jan.	28—J. D. Turner, St. Louis	W	10
Feb.	13—Tony Zale, New York	W	12

1943-1944
(Inactive)

1945

Oct.	29—Bearcat Jones, Cleveland	Exh.	3
Nov.	7—Bearcat Jones, Kansas City	Exh.	3

1946

June	19—Joe Louis, New York	KO by	8
	(For World Heavyweight Title)		

1947
(Inactive)

1948

Nov	15—Mike O'Dowd, Macon ....,...	KO	9
Nov	25—Jackie Lyons, Dallas	KO	9
Dec.	10—Joe Louis, Chicago	Exh.	6

TB	KO	WD	WF	D	LD	LF	KO BY	ND	NC
75	14	49	0	1	9	0	2	0	0

Elected to Boxing Hall of Fame. 1965

JOE LOUIS' RECORD

JOE LOUIS
(Joseph Louis Barrow)
(The Brown Bomber)
Born, May 13, 1914, Lafayette, Alabama. Weight,
181-218 lbs. Height, 6 ft. 1¾ in. Managed by Julian Black
and John Roxoborough; later by Marshall Miles
1934 National AAU Light Heavyweight Champion

1934

Date	Opponent	Result	Rd
July	4—Jack Kracken, Chicago	KO	1
July	11—Willie Davis, Chicago	KO	3
July	29—Larry Udell, Chicago	KO	2
Aug.	13—Jack Kranz, Chicago	W	8
Aug.	27—Buck Everett, Chicago	KO	2
Sept.	11—Alex Borchuk, Detroit	KO	4
Sept.	25—Adolph Wiater, Chicago	W	10
Oct.	24—Art Sykes, Chicago	KO	8
Oct.	30—Jack O'Dowd, Detroit	KO	2
Nov.	14—Stanley Poreda, Chicago	KO	1
Nov.	30—Charley Massera, Chicago	KO	3
Dec.	14—Lee Ramage, Chicago	KO	8

1935

Date	Opponent	Result	Rd
Jan.	4—Patsy Perroni, Detroit	W	10
Jan.	11—Hans Birkie, Pittsburgh	KO	10
Feb.	21—Lee Ramage, Los Angeles	KO	2
Mar.	8—Donald (Reds) Barry, San Francisco	KO	3
Mar.	29—Natie Brown, Detroit	W	10
Apr.	12—Roy Lazer, Chicago	KO	3
Apr.	22—Biff Benton, Dayton	KO	2
Apr.	27—Roscoe Toles, Flint	KO	6
May	3—Willie Davis, Peoria	KO	2
May	7—Gene Stanton, Kalamazoo	KO	3
June	25—Primo Carnera, New York	KO	6
Aug.	7—King Levinsky, Chicago	KO	1
Sept.	24—Max Baer, New York	KO	4
Dec.	14—Paulino Uzcudun, New York	KO	4

1936

Date	Opponent	Result	Rd
Jan.	17—Charley Retzlaff, Chicago	KO	1
June	19—Max Schmeling, New York	KO by	12
Aug.	18—Jack Sharkey, New York	KO	3
Sept.	22—Al Ettore, Philadelphia	KO	5
Oct.	9—Jorge Brescia, New York	KO	3
Oct.	14—Willie Davis, South Bend	Exh. KO	3
Oct.	14—K.O. Brown, South Bend	Exh. KO	3
Nov.	20—Paul Williams, New Orleans	Exh. KO	2
Nov.	20—Tom Jones, New Orleans	Exh. KO	3
Dec.	14—Eddie Simms, Cleveland	KO	1

1937

Date	Opponent	Result	Rd
Jan.	11—Stanley Ketchell, Buffalo	Exh. KO	2
Jan.	29—Bob Pastor, New York	W	10
Feb.	17—Natie Brown, Kansas City	KO	4
June	22—James J. Braddock, Chicago	KO	8
	(Won World Heavyweight Title)		
Aug.	30—Tommy Farr, New York	W	15
	(Retained World Heavyweight Title)		

1938

Date	Opponent	Result	Rd
Feb.	23—Nathan Mann, New York	KO	3
	(Retained WOrld Heavy Weight Title)		

Apr.	1—Harry Thomas, Chicago .... KO	5
	(Retained World Heavyweight Title)	
June	22—Max Schmeling, New York .... KO	1
	(Retained World Heavyweight Title)	

1939

Jan.	25—John Henry Lewis, New York .... KO	1
	(Retained World Heavyweight Title)	
Apr.	17—Jack Roper, Los Angeles .... KO	1
	(Retained World Heavyweight Title)	
June	28—Tony Galento, New York .... KO	4
	(Retained World Heavyweight Title)	
Sept.	20—Bob Pastor, Detroit .... KO	11
	(Retained World Heavyweight Title)	

1940

Feb.	9—Arturo Godoy, New York .... W	15
	(Retained Heavyweight Title)	
Mar.	29—Johnny Paychek, New York ...... KO	2
	(Retained World Heavyweight Title)	
June	20—Arturo Godoy, New York .... KO	8
	(Retained World Heavyweight Title)	
Dec.	16—Al McCoy, Boston .... KO	6
	(Retained World Heavyweight Title)	

1941

Jan.	31—Red Burman, New York .... KO	5
	(Retained World Heavyweight Title)	
Feb.	17—Gus Dorazio, Philadelphia .... KO	2
	(Retained World Heavyweight Title)	
Mar.	21—Abe Simon, Detroit .... KO	13
	(Retained World Heavyweight Title)	
Apr.	8—Tony Musto, St. Louis .... KO	9
	(Retained World Heavyweight Title)	
May	23—Buddy Baer, Washington, D.C. W disq.	7
	(Retained World Heavyweight Title)	
June	18—Billy Conn, New York .... KO	13
	(Retained World Heavyweight Title)	
July	11—Jim Robinson, Minneapolis .. Exh. KO	1
Sept.	29—Lou Nova, New York.............. KO	6
	(Retained World Heavyweight Title)	
Nov.	25—George Giambastiani, Los Angeles Exh.	4

1942

Jan.	9—Buddy Baer, New York .... KO	1
	(Retained World Heavyweight Title)	
Mar.	27—Abe Simon, New York .... KO	6
	(Retained World Heavyweight Title)	
June	5—George Nicholson, Fort Hamilton Exh.	3

1943

(Inactive)

1944

Nov.	3—Johnny Demson, Detroit .... Exh. KO	2
Nov.	6—Charley Crump, Baltimore ...... Exh.	3
Nov.	9—Dee Amos, Hartford .... Exh.	3
Nov.	13—Jimmy Bell, Washington, D.C. ... Exh.	3
Nov.	14—Johnny Davis, Buffalo .... Exh. KO	1
Nov.	15—Dee Amos, Elizabeth .... Exh.	3
Nov.	17—Dee Amos, Camden .... Exh.	3
Nov.	24—Dan Merritt, Chicago .... Exh.	3

1945

Nov.	15—Sugar Lip Anderson. San Francisco .... Exh.	2
Nov.	15—Big Boy Brown, San Francisco ... Exh.	2
Nov.	29—Big Boy Brown, Sacramento ..... Exh.	2

Nov.	29—Bobby Lee, Sacramento .... Exh.	2
Dec.	10—Bob Frazier, Victoria .... Exh.	3
Dec.	11—Big Boy Brown, Portland .... Exh.	2
Dec.	11—Dave Johnson, Portland .... Exh.	2
Dec.	12—Big Boy Brown, Eugene .... Exh.	3
Dec.	13—Big Boy Brown, Vancouver ...... Exh.	3

1946

June	19—Billy Conn, New York .... KO	8
	(Retained World Heavyweight Title)	
Sept.	18—Tami Mauriello, New York .... KO	1
	(Retained World Heavyweight Title)	
Nov.	11—Cleo Everett, Honolulu .... Exh.	4
Nov.	11—Wayne Powell, Honolulu .... Exh.	2
Nov.	25—Perk Daniels, Mexicali .... Exh.	4

1947

Feb.	7—Arturo Godoy, Mexico City ...... Exh.	10
Dec.	5—Jersey Joe Walcott, New York ..... W	15
	(Retained World Heavyweight Title)	

1948

June	25—Jersey Joe Walcott, New York .... KO	11
	(Retained World Heavyweight Title)	

1949

Mar.	1—Announced retirement.	

1950

Sept.	27—Ezzard Charles, New York L	15
	(For World Heavyweight Title)	
Nov.	29—Cesar Brion, New York .... W	10

1951

Jan.	3—Freddie Beshore, Detroit .... KO	4
Feb.	7—Omelio Agramonte, Miami .... W	10
Feb.	23—Andy Walker, San Francisco ..... KO	10
May	2—Omelio Agramonte, Detroit .... W	10
June	15—Lee Savold, New York .... KO	6
Aug.	1—Cesar Brion, San Francisco .... W	10
Aug.	15—Jimmy Bivins, Baltimore .... W	10
Oct.	26—Rocky Marciano, New York ... KO by	8

TB	KO	WD	WF	D	LD	LF	KO BY	ND	NC
70	53	13	1	0	1	0	2	0	0

Elected to Boxing Hall of Fame, 1954.
Died, April 12, 1981, Las Vegas, Nevada.

FORMER WORLD CHAMPIONS

EDDIE (BABE) RISKO
(Henry L. Pylkowski)
Born, July 14, 1911, Syracuse, N.Y. Ancestry,
Polish-Lithuanian. Weight, 160 lbs. Height, 5 ft. 10 in.
Managed by Gabe Genovese.
Fought as "Henry Pulaski," 1932-34.

1932

Apr.	14—Joe Smallwood, Philadelphia	W	6
Sept.	16—Harry Walton, San Diego	D	4
Nov.	4—Tony Pena, San Diego	W	4

1933

Jan.	13—Jack O'Neil, San Diego	W	6
Mar.	3—Guy McKinney, San Diego	W	6
Mar.	10—Grant Willardson, San Diego	LF	3
May	19—Guy McKinney, San Diego	KO	5
June	15—Miles Murphy, Tacoma	KO	6
Aug.	4—Fay Griffiths, San Diego	KO	3
Aug.	18—Johnny Carvos, San Diego	KO	6
Sept.	3—Dutch Weimer, Tijuana	L	4
Sept.	22—Leo Kelly, San Diego	W	6
Oct.	20—Johnny (Bandit) Romero, San Diego	W	10
Dec.	8—Nick Urez, San Diego	KO	3

1934

Jan.	12—Swede Berglund, San Diego ..	KO by	4
Mar.	16—Steve Wolanin, Utica	W	8
May	7—Jackie Flowers, Syracuse	W	6
May	15—Bucky Lawless, Syracuse	W	6
June	12—Bucky Lawless, Binghamton	KO	5
July	18—Paulie Sykes, Oswego	D	6
July	29—Joe Desmond, Saratoga	W	6
Aug.	9—Larry Wagner, Johnson City	D	6
Sept.	10—Werner Wilsch, Syracuse	KO	2
Sept.	17—Pete Suskey, Syracuse	W	6
Oct.	15—Freddie Sallus, Syracuse	D	8
Oct.	29—Werner Wilsch, Binghamton	KO	3
Nov.	5—Freddie Sallus, Syracuse	KO	8
Nov.	19—Al Sabano, Syracuse	W	10
Nov.	26—Chester Palutis, Scranton	W	6
Dec.	12—Pete Suskey, Scranton	W	6

1935

Jan.	1—Teddy Yarosz, Scranton	KO	7
Jan.	25—Vince Dundee, New York	L	10
Jan.	29—Solly Dukelsky, Chicago	D	10
Feb.	25—Paul Pirrone, Philadelphia	W	10
Mar.	11—Benny Levine, Syracuse	KO	2
Mar.	18—Sammy Slaughter, Philadelphia ...	W	10
Mar.	25—Jimmy Belmont, Cleveland	L	8
May.	22—Frank Battaglia, Pittsburgh	W	10
July	8—Paul Pirrone, Cleveland	L	10
Sept.	19—Teddy Yarosz, Pittsburgh	W	15
(Won NBA-New York World Middleweight Title)			
Oct.	4—Jackie Aldare, Syracuse	W	10
Oct.	21—Chester Palutis, Scranton	W	10
Dec.	9—Frank Battaglia, Philadelphia	W	10
Dec.	20—Jock McAvoy, New York	KO by	1

1936

Feb.	10—Tony Fisher, Newark	W	15

(Retained NBA-New York World Middleweight Title)

Mar.	24—Freddie Steele, Seattle	L	10
Apr.	9—Mike Payan, San Diego	W	10
May	8—Fred Apostoli, San Francisco	L	10
July	11—Freddie Steele, Seattle	L	15

(Lost NBA-New York World Middleweight Title)

Sept.	21—Teddy Yarosz, Pittsburgh	L	10
Oct.	28—Harry Balsamo, New York	W	10
Nov.	27—Tony Tozzo, Buffalo	W	10
Dec.	18—Joe (Butch) Lynch, Syracuse	KO	8

1937

Feb.	19—Freddie Steele, New York	L	15

(For NBA-New York World Middleweight Title)

Mar.	11—Billy Conn, Pittsburgh	L	10
July	13—Al Hostak, Seattle	KO by	7
Aug.	17—George Black, Milwaukee	KO by	5

1938

May	10—Gorilla Jones, Akron	W	10
June	6—Al Quaill, Pittsburgh	D	10
June	27—Ralph DeJohn, Syracuse	KO by	7
July	18—Ben Brown, Atlanta	D	10
Sept.	17—Larry Lane, Trenton	KO by	2
Sept.	26—Ben Brown, Atlanta	KO by	9
Oct.	5—Billy Soose, Pittsburgh	KO by	3

1939

Feb.	7—Walter Franklin, New York ...	KO by	6
May	17—Lloyd Marshall, Sacramento ...	KO by	5

TB	KO	WD	WF	D	LD	LF	KO BY	ND	NC
66	12	26	0	7	10	1	10	0	0

Died, March 7, 1957, Syracuse, N.Y.

TEDDY YAROSZ
**Born, June 24, 1910, Pittsburgh, Pa.
Nationality, Polish-American. Weight, 158 lbs.
Height, 5 ft. 10 in. Managed by Ray Foutts.**

1929
Knockouts: Jack McCarthy, 2; Johnny
**Judd, 4; Carl Patron, 5; Johnny Dill, 5. Won:
Jackie King, 4; Johnny Brown, 6; Young Joe
Wolcott, 6; Georgie Bretch, 6; Bob Collura, 6;
Billy Yeltz, 6; Johnny Brown, 6; Billy Holt, 6.**

1930
Knockouts: Billy Burke, 2; Jimmie
Herman, 3; Jack Murphy, 8; Benny Burns, 5.
Won: Johnny Ponoic, 6; Jackie Herman, 6;
Jimmie McGraw, 6; Hans Roberts, 10; Young
Joe Wolcott, 8; Paul Ogre, 10; Young Rudy, 10;
Joe Corelli, 8; Paul Ogre, 6; Young Rudy, 10;
Jackie Herman, 10; Roger Brooks, 10; Joe
Randall, 10; Jimmie Neal, 10; Young Billy
Holt, 10; Johnny Rich, 10; Tiger Rudy, 10.

1931
Jan.	13—Jimmie Moinette, Alliance, O. .	W 10
Jan.	20—Jimmie Belmont, Oil City, Pa. .	W 10
Jan.	30—Mickey Fedor, E. Liverpool, O.	W 10
Feb.	6—Larry Madge, Franklin, Pa. . . .	W 8
Feb.	21—Tiger Joe Randall, Pittsburgh .	W 10
Mar.	16—Joe Trippe, Oil City, Pa.	W 10
Mar.	23—Eddie Kaufman, Canton, O. .	KO 4
Apr.	8—Larry Madge, Oil City, Pa.	W 10
Apr.	16—Tiger Joe Randall, McKeesport, Pa.	W 10
June	2—Tommy Rios, E. Liverpool, O.	W 10
July	9—Buck McTiernan, Pittsburgh . .	W 10
July	16—Marty McHale, Parkersburg, W. Va.	W 10
July	27—Bucky Lawless, Pittsburgh . . .	W 10
Aug.	20—Tiger Joe Randall, Pittsburgh .	W 10
Dec.	10—Jimmie Moinette, East Liverpool Ohio	W 10
Dec.	25—Jimmy Belmont, Pittsburgh . .	W 10

1932
Jan.	22—Jimmy Hill, Detroit	W 10
Apr.	11—Vincent Hambright, Pittsburgh	W 10
June	30—Johnny Hayes, Pittsburgh . . .	KO 8
July	22—Lope Tenorio, Pittsburgh . . .	W 10
Aug.	12—Eddie Kid Wolfe, Detroit	W 10
Aug.	30—Jimmy Belmont, Pittsburgh . .	W 10
Oct.	7—Eddie Kid Wolfe, N. Y. C.	D 10
Oct.	14—Abe Lichtenstein, Pittsburgh . .	W 10
Nov.	18—Jack King, Pittsburgh	W 10
Dec.	9—Jack King, Pittsburgh	W 10

1933
Jan.	23—Eddie Kid Wolfe, Pittsburgh . .	L 10
Feb.	27—Eddie Kid Wolfe, Pittsburgh . .	D 10
Mar.	10—Eddie Ran, Detroit	W 10
Mar.	24—Paulie Walker, Pittsburgh . . .	W 10
Apr.	10—Andy Divodi, Pittsburgh	KO 5
May	22—Tommy Freeman, Pittsburgh .	W 10
June	20—Sammy Slaughter, Cleveland . .	W 10
July	24—Freddie Polo, Newark	KO 5
Aug.	1—Al Rossi, Newark	W 10
Aug.	21—Vince Dundee, Pittsburgh . . .	W 10
Sept.	18—Vince Dundee, Newark	W 10
Oct.	25—Young Terry, Newark	L 10
Dec.	4—Paul Pirrone, Cleveland	W 10
Dec.	11—Tony D'Allesandro, Holyoke .	W 10

1934
Feb.	12—Jimmy Smith, Pittsburgh	W 15
Apr.	6—Ben Jeby, Pittsburgh	W 12
Apr.	16—Tommy Rios, Canton	W 10
May	18—Freddie Heinz, Clarksburg	W 10

June	5—Pete Latzo, Pittsburgh	KO	4
July	18—Tait Littman, Chicago	W	10
Aug.	13—Bud Saltis, E. Liverpool	W	10
Sept.	11—Vince Dundee, Pittsburgh	W	15
	(Won American Middleweight Title)		
Oct.	29—Johnny Phagan, Milwaukee ...	W	10
Dec.	14—Kid Leonard, Chicago	W	10

1935

Jan.	1—Babe Risko, Scranton ...	KO by	7
July	30—Fred Sallus, Steubenville	KO	2
Sept.	2—Oscar Schmeling, Louisville ..	KO	3
Sept.	19—Babe Risko, Pittsburgh	L	15
	(Lost American Middleweight Title)		

1936

May	19—Bob Turner, Pittsburgh	W	10
Aug.	13—Young Terry, Youngstown ..	KO	10
Sept.	21—Babe Risko, Pittsburgh	W	10
Nov.	4—Ken Overlin, Pittsburgh	W	10
Dec.	17—Eddie Maguire, Pittsburgh	W	10

1937

Jan.	13—Solly Krieger, N. Y. C.	W	10
May	7—Lou Brouillard, Boston	W	10
June	30—Billy Conn, Pittsburgh	L	12
Sept.	30—Billy Conn, Pittsburgh	L	15
Dec.	9—Carmelo Candel, Paris	L	10

1938

Feb.	7—Paulie Mahoney, Buffalo	W	10
Mar.	28—Carmen Barth, Cleveland	L	10
Apr.	26—George Black, Milwaukee	W	10
May	18—Al Quaill, Pittsburgh	W	10
June	6—Georgie Abrams, Wash., D. C. .	L	10
July	25—Billy Conn, Pittsburgh	W	12
Sept.	13—Jimmy Clark, Rochester	W	10
Oct.	21—Oscar Rankins, Pittsburgh	W	10
Nov.	1—Ralph DeJohn, Rochester	W	10
Nov.	11—Ralph DeJohn, Rochester	L	10
Dec.	12—Ralph DeJohn, Rochester	W	10

1939

Feb.	3—Eric Seelig, N. Y. C.	D	8
Mar.	27—Ken Overlin, Houston	W	10
Apr.	20—Archie Moore, St. Louis	W	10
July	17—Al Gainer, Pittsburgh	W	10
Aug.	9—Ben Brown, Atlanta	L	10
Sept.	11—Ben Brown, Atlanta	L	10
Sept.	29—Lloyd Marshall, San Francisco	L	10

1940

Jan.	8—Nate Bolden, Pittsburgh	W	10
Feb.	29—Willie Muldoon, Cleveland	W	10
Mar.	26—Turkey Thompson, Los Ang. .	L	10
Apr.	15—Jimmy Reeves, Cleveland	W	10
June	27—Bud Mignault, E. Liverpool ...	W	10
Oct.	21—Lloyd Marshall, Pittsburgh ...	W	10

1941

Mar.	5—Jimmy Bivins, Cleveland	L	10
Mar.	26—Bob Berry, Akron	W	10
June	16—Tommy Gomez, Tampa	L	10
June	30—Jimmy Young, Johnstown ...	W	10
Nov.	17—Ezzard Charles, Cincinnati ...	L	10

1942

Feb.	12—Joe Muscato, Rochester	L	8

TB	KO	WD	WF	D	LD	LF	KOBY	ND	NC
127	16	90	0	3	17	0	1	0	0

Died, March 29, 1974, Monaca, Pa.

FRITZIE ZIVIC

Born, May 8, 1913. Pittsburgh. Nationality, Croatian-American. Height, 5 ft. 9 in.
Managed by Luke Carney.

1931

Knockouts: Al Reddinger, 1. Lost: Steve
Senich, 6.

1932

Knockouts: Pat Gilmore, 1; Elmer Kozack,
4; Jimmy Dorsey, 4; Terry Waner, 3. Won:
Young Lowsteter, 6; Eddie Cregan, 4. Lost:
Steve Senich, 6; Jerry Clements, 6.

1933

Jan.	30—Georgie Schley, Pittsburgh	...KO	2
Feb.	8—Steve Senich, Pittsburgh	......KO	2
Mar.	24—U. S. Carpentier, Pittsburgh	...KO	4
Apr.	10—Eddie Brannon, Pittsburgh	...KO	6
Apr.	28—Patsy Henningan, Pittsburgh	... W	6
June	26—Don Asto, Pittsburgh	.... W	6
July	10—Don Asto, Pittsburgh	........KO	3
Aug.	7—Joey Greb, Millsdale, Pa.	...... W	10
Oct.	12—Joe Pimenthal, Pasadena	.....KO	4
Nov.	3—Gus Vagas, San Francisco	.....KO	2
Nov.	23—Don Miller, Pasadena	........KO	3
Dec.	4—Homer Foster, Pico, Cal.	...... D	4
Dec.	15—Vincent Martinez, Hollywood	. W	4
Dec.	27—Rudy Ayon, Pico, Cal.	.... W	4

1934

Jan.	5—Louis Carranza, Los Angeles	... W	6
Jan.	30—Lloyd Smith, Los Angeles	..... D	6
Feb.	22—Perfecto Lopez, Los Angeles	... W	6
Mar.	5—Lloyd Smith, Los Angeles	..... D	6
July	2—Eddie Ran, Pittsburgh	.... W	10
July	25—Young Joe Firpo Conneaut Lake, Pa.	.... W	8
Sept.	2—Harry Carlton, Pittsburgh	..... W	10
Oct.	25—Laddie Tonelli, Chicago	... KO by	3

1935

Feb.	4—Jimmy Leto, Holyoke	L	10
Feb.	18—Johnny Jadick, Washington	L	10
Mar.	10—Kayo Castillo, Holyoke	.... W	10
Mar.	25—Dom Mancini, Pittsburgh	...... D	10
Apr.	2—Dom Mancini, Pittsburgh	......KO	11
Apr.	16—Marty Gornick, Steubenville	..KO	5
May	15—Freddy Chenowyth, Chicago	.. W	8
May	30—Eddie Adams, Kent	.........KO	6
June	4—Sammy Chivas, Chicago	......KO	3
July	1—Lou Ambers, Pittsburgh	L	10
July	15—Jackie McFarland, Millvale	.... W	10
Aug.	1—Mike Barto, Millvale	.... W	12
Aug.	8—Joey Ferrando, Jersey City	L	10
Sept.	30—Tony Herrera, Pittsburgh	L	10
Oct.	4—George Salvadore, N. Y. C.	L	6
Dec.	16—Billy Celebron, Chicago	L	10

1936

Jan.	13—Eddie Cool, Pittsburgh	L	10
Jan.	27—Joey Ferando, N. Y.	L	8
Feb.	24—Chuck Woods, Pittsburgh	L	10
Apr.	15—Joe Flocco, Harrisburg	......Exh.	10
Apr.	27—Gene Buffalo, Atlantic City	L	10
May	22—Billy Celebron, St. Louis	.....KO	1
June	9—Tony Falco, Pittsburgh	.......KO	8
June	27—Al Manfredo, St. Louis	.... W	10
July	2—Lou Jallos, Steubenville	......KO	10
July	6—Laddie Tonelli, Pittsburgh	....KO	4
July	22—Mickey Duris, Johnstown	.... W	12
July	30—Laddie Tonelli, Pittsburgh	....KO	6
Aug.	12—Cleto Locatelli, Brooklyn	L	10
Sept.	28—Jackie McFarland, Canton	..... W	10

```
Oct.    5—Johnny Durso, Pittsburgh ....KO   2
Oct.   16—Chuck Woods, St. Louis ......KO   6
Nov.    9—Gaston LeCadre, Pittsburgh ...W  10
Dec.    2—Harry Dublinsky, Pittsburgh ..KO  6
Dec.   28—Billy Conn, Pittsburgh ........L  10
                    1937
Feb.   11—Johnny Jadick, Pittsburgh ....KO  6
Mar.    1—Bobby Pacho, Pittsburgh ......W  10
Apr.    6—Chuck Woods, Detroit ........W  10
May    21—Tony Petrowski, Muskegon ....W  10
Oct.   29—Frankie Portland,
           Clarksb'h, W. Va. ..............KO  2
Nov.   18—Jimmy Reilly, McKeespt., Pa...KO  1
Dec.   25—Tommy Bland, Pittsburgh ......L  10
                    1938
Jan.    7—Harold Brown, Chicago .......W  10
Feb.   14—Frankie Blair, Pittsburgh ......W  10
Mar.    7—Tommy Bland, Pittsburgh ....KO  8
Mar.   21—Charlie Burley, Pittsburgh .....W  10
Apr.   12—Remo Fernandez, Detroit .....W  10
May    29—Petey Mike, Brooklyn ........KO  1
June   13—Charlie Burley, Pittsburgh .....L  10
June   20—Ercole Buratti, Pittsburgh ....KO  4
July    9—Eddie Connley, Walnut Beach .KO  6
July   12—Phil Furr, Pittsburgh .........KO  3
Aug.    2—Joe Lemieux, Newark ........KO  4
Aug.   12—Joe Pennino, Coney Island .....W  8
Aug.   22—Steve Kahley, Newark ........KO  3
Aug.   26—Mickey Paul, Lg. Beach, L.I. ..KO  3
Sept.  13—Bobby Pacho, Newark ........W  10
Oct.    3—Paul Cortlyn, Newark ........KO  4
Oct.   10—Jay Macedon, Newark ........KO  5
Oct.   27—Salvy Sabin, Pittsburgh ........W  10
Nov.   15—Frankie Blair, N. Y. C. ........W  8
Nov.   21—Al Hamilton, Columbus ......KO  5
Dec.    7—Vincent Pimpinella, Pittsburgh . W  10
Dec.   26—Howell King, Toledo .......... D  10
                    1939
Jan.     —Al Costello, Columbus, Ohio ..KO  2
Jan.   20—Jackie Burke, St. Louis ........W  10
Feb.   10—Eddie Booker, N. Y. C. ........W  8
Feb.   15—Charlie Bell, Columbus ..:....KO  3
Mar.   20—Nick Pastore, Miami .........KO  9
Mar.   29—Bobby Britton, Miami .........W  10
Apr.   20—Tiger Walker, St. Louis .......KO  1
May     9—Kenny La Salle, Houston ......L  10
May    16—Al Traino, Rochester ..........W  10
June    5—Kenny La Salle, Pittsburgh ....W  10
July   11—Jackie Burke, St. Louis ........W  10
July   17—Charley Burley, Pittsburgh .....L  10
Sept.   5—Pete De Ruzza, Pittsburgh ....KO  6
Sept.  12—Ralph Gizzy, McKeesport, Pa. KO  2
Oct.   24—Kid Azteca, Houston ..........W  10
Oct.   30—Milo Theodorescu, Pittsburgh.. W  10
Nov.   18—Billy Lancaster, Brooklyn ....KO  7
Dec.    9—Wicky Harkins, Philadelphia ..KO  9
Dec.   27—Milt Aron, Chicago .......KO by  8
                    1940
Jan.   22—Mike Kaplan, Philadelphia .....W  10
Mar.    4—Saverio Turiello, Philadelphia .KO  1
Mar.    7—Remo Fernandez, Cleveland ..KO  7
Mar.   14—Johnny Barbara, Chicago ......W  10
Apr.    8—Johnny Barbara, Philadelphia ...L  10


May     3—Mansfield Driskell, Detroit ....W  10
May     7—Johnny Barbara, Philadelphia ...L  10
May    21—Ossie Harris, Pittsburgh ......KO  3
June   24—Johnny Rinaldi, Pittsburgh ...KO  1
July    8—Ossie Harris, Pittsburgh .......W  10
July   22—Leonard Bennett, Chicago ....KO  4
```

91

```
Aug.    5—Kenny La Salle, Pittsburgh  .... W   10
Aug.   28—Sammy Angott, Pittsburgh  .... W   10
Oct.    4—Henry Armstrong, N. Y. C.  .... W   15
            (Won Welterweight Title)
Nov.   15—Al Davis, N. Y. C. ........ W Disq.   2
Nov.   26—Ronnie Beaudin, Buffalo ..... KO   2
Dec.   20—Lew Jenkins, N. Y. C. ......... D   10
                     1941
Jan.   17—Henry Armstrong, N. Y. C. ...KO   12
            (Title Match)
Mar.   17—Saverio Turiello, Pittsburgh.... W   10
Mar.   20—Felix Garcia, Baltimore ...... KO   2
Apr.    4—Dick Demeray, Minneapolis ..KO   5
Apr.   18—Mike Kaplan, Boston ...........L   10
May     2—Tony Martellano, N. Y. C. ...... W   10
July    2—Al Davis, N. Y. C. .......... W   10
July   14—Johnny Barbara, Philadelphia .. W   12
July   29—Freddie Red Cochrane, Newark .L   15
            (Lost Welterweight Championship)
Sept.  15—Milt Aron, Pittsburgh ........ KO   5
Oct.   31—Ray Robinson, N. Y. C. .......L   10
Nov.   26—Phil Furr, Wash., D. C. .......... W   10
Dec.    1—Harry Weekly, Cleveland ..... KO   9
Dec.   12—Young Kid McCoy, N. Y. C..... D   10
                     1942
Jan.   16—Ray Robinson, N. Y. C. ...KO by  10
Feb.    9—Raul Carrabantes, Pittsburgh .. W   10
Feb.   27—Tony Motisi, Chicago .........L   10
Mar.    9—Izzy Jannazzo, Pittsburgh ....KO   5
Mar.   30—Wild Bill McDowell, Newark ..KO   6
Apr.   13—Maxie Berger, Pittsburgh ...... W   10
Apr.   23—Ruben Shank, Minneapolis .....L   10
May    25—Lew Jenkins, Pittsburgh ...... KO   10
June    4—Reuben Shank, Minneapolis ... W   10
June   22—Bobby Dutton, Wilkes-Barre ..KO   4
June   29—Norman Rubio, Newark .......L   10
July   27—Norman Rubio, Pittsburgh ...KO   9
Aug.   13—Garvey Young, N. Y. C. ...... KO   6
Sept.  10—Freddie Cochrane, N. Y. C. .... W   10
Sept.  21—Johnny Walker, Philadelphia ... W   10
Oct.   13—Tito Taylor, Milwaukee ....... W   10
Oct.   26—Henry Armstrong, San Fran.....L   10
Nov.   16—Sheik Rangel, San Fran. .......L   10
Dec.   15—Carmen Notch, Pittsburgh ..... W   10
                     1943
Feb.    5—Beau Jack, N. Y. C. ............L   10
Feb.   16—Mayon Padlo, Pittsburgh ...... W   10
Mar.    5—Beau Jack, N. Y. C. ............L   12
Apr.   30—Johnny Roszina, Milwaukee ..KO   8
June   10—Jake LaMotta, Pittsburgh ......L   10
July   12—Jake LaMotta, Pittsburgh ...... W   15
Aug.    9—Kid McCoy, Pittsburgh .......KO   4
Aug.   23—Bob Montgomery, Philadelphia .L   10
Sept.  10—Vinnie Vines, N. Y. C. .........KO   1
Oct.   15—Jose Basora, Detroit ...........L   10
Oct.   29—Bobby Richardson, Chicago ... W   10
Nov.   12—Jake LaMotta, N. Y. C. .........L   10
Dec.   20—Ralph Zanelli, Boston ..........L   10
                     1944
Jan.    3—Ossie Harris, Pittsburgh ...... KO   10
Jan.   14—Jake LaMotta, Detroit .........L   10
Mar.   27—Harry Teaney, Milwaukee ..... W   10
Mar.   29—Freddie Archer, Elizabeth ......L   10
June   26—Tommy Bell, Pittsburgh ........L   10
            In U. S. Army.
Aug.    1—Pete DeRuzza, Houston ...... KO   8
Sept.  12—Felix Morales, San Antonio ...KO   2
Sept.  26—Artie Dorrell, Galveston ...... KO   7
Oct.   16—Tommy Roman, Shreveport ....L   10
Oct.   18—Pete Saia, Dallas ..............KO   8
```

92

Nov. 14—PFC Chuck Hirst, Houston ...KO 5
Nov. 29—Manuel Villa, Dallas..........KO 6
Dec. 12—Kid Azteca, San Antonio ...... W 10
1945
Jan.   5—Billy Arnold, New York .... W 8
Feb. 22—Kid Astrada, Camp Maxey ....KO 2
Mar.   6—Bill McDowell, Galveston ...... W 10
Mar. 22—Ben Evans, Galveston ....KO 8
Apr.   3—Manuel Villa, San Antonio ....KO 8
May   7—Kid Azteca, San Antonio ...... W 10
May   8—Pat Saia, Beaumont .... W 10
June 12—Baby Zavala, San Antonio ....KO 4
June 22—Harold Green, New York ....L 10
July   3—Ruben Shank, Pittsburgh ....L 10
July 10—Ossie Harris, Pittsburgh ....L 10
July 16—Bill McDowell, New Orleans ....L 10
Sept. 12—Paul Altman, Houston .... L 10
Sept. 18—Billy Derg, Oklahoma City .... L 10
Oct. 20—Joe Reddick, New York ....L 10
Nov.   2—Freddie Archer, New York ....L 10
Nov. 13—Joe Curcio, Elizabeth ....L 10
Dec. 10—Cecil Hudson, New York ....L 10
1946
Jan. 15—Al (Red) Priest, Boston ....L 10
Feb.   1—O'Neil Bell, Detroit ....L 10
Feb. 25—Aaron Perry, Wash., D.C........L 10
Mar. 19—Levi Southall, Kansas City .....W 10
Mar. 26—Tony Elizondo, San Antonio ...L 10
Apr.   5—Manuel Villa, El Paso .... D 10
Apr. 12—Lincoln Stanley, Portland, Ore. W 10
Apr. 18—Don Lee, Hollywood .... W 10
Apr. 29—Howard Blyhl, Omaha .... W 10
May   1—Joey Martinez, Wichita ....KO 8
May 14—Jackie Wilson, Los Angeles .....L 10
May 27—Tommy Lemmon, Milwaukee ...L 10
Oct. 29—Russell Wilmite, Memphis .....KO 5
Nov. 12—Al Mobley, Trenton ....L 8
Nov. 18—Jimmy McGriff, Wash. .... D 10
Dec.   2—Ralph Zannelli, Providence .....L 10
Dec.   6—Pete Mead, Grand Rapids ....L 10
Dec. 10—Bobby Britton, Memphis ...... W 10
1947
Jan.   8—Clyde Gordon, Miami ....L 10
Feb. 15—Kid Azteca, Mexico City ..KO by 5
1948
Oct. 28—Eddie Steele, Macon, Ga. ...... D 10
1949
Jan. 12—Al Reid, Macon, Ga. .... W 10
Jan. 17—Eddie Steele, Augusta .... W 10

TB	KO	WD	WF	D	LD	LF	KOBY	ND	NC
230	80	74	1	10	61	0	4	0	0

Elected to Hall of Fame in 1972

SOLLY KREIGER

Born, March 28, 1909, New York City, N.Y. Weight, 160 lbs. Height, 5 ft. 8 in. Managed by Hymie Caplan.

1928
Dec.	22—Lee Page, New York	W	4

1929
Feb.	1—Con Cordero, New York	W	4
Mar.	11—Duffy Moore, Brooklyn	KO	3
Apr.	20—Artie Carr, New York	KO	4
May	13—Manny Davis, New York	D	6
July	19—Eddie McLaughlin, Long Beach	W	6
Aug.	9—Joe Gorman, Long Beach	W	6
	—Jose Rodriguez, Long Beach	D	6
Oct.	7—Rosen Brito, New York	KO	3
Oct.	28—Willie Young, New York	KO	2
Dec.	2—Pete Horton, New York	W	6
Dec.	23—Eddie Forster, New York	KO	3

1930
Feb.	28—Marco Appicello, New York	W	4
Mar.	21—Freddie Kelly, New York	KO	1
May	12—Steve Gotch, New York	KO	3
May	26—Joel LaGrey, New York	L	6
Aug.	16—Billy Drako, Long Beach	KO	1
Nov.	4—Billy Tosk, New York	W	4
Dec.	2—Billy DeJanis, New York	KO	2

1931
June	15—Joe Gorman, New York	D	8
June	24—Mickey Marino, Long Beach	W	8
July	13—Joel LaGrey, New York	W	8
Aug.	7—Larry Marinucci, Canarsie	W	6
Aug.	27—Hans Mueller, New York	W	8
Sept.	17—My Sullivan, New York	D	10
Oct.	16—Vince Dundee, New York	KO by	8

1932
	—George Cherubini, Fort Hamilton	KO	2
July	28—Walter Braun, Fort Hamilton	KO	3
Nov.	22—Red Gregory, Los Angeles	KO	4
Dec.	6—Ray Acosta, Los Angeles	KO	1
Dec.	30—Jimmy Evans, Hollywood	W	10

1933
Mar.	4—Larry Marinucci, Brooklyn	W	6
Mar.	17—Connie Josenio, New York	KO	2
Apr.	3—Jay Macedon, Newark	KO	7
Apr.	17—Pete Susky, Newark	W	10
	—Jackie Aldare, New York	L	6
June	13—Al Rossi, Newark	L	10
Aug.	7—Al Diamond, Newark	W	10
	—Eddie Whalen, New York	KO	2
	—Frank Fullam, New York	W	6
	—Vincent Serici, New York	D	8

1934
May	18—Swede Berglund, San Diego	L	10
	—Ray Acosta	KO	3

1935
June	20—Tony Celli, New York	KO	2
July	4—Eddie Whalen, New York	KO	1
July	24—Al Rossi, New York	KO	6
Aug.	12—Tony Fisher, Newark	W	10
Sept.	30—Ray Miller, Newark	KO	6
Oct.	8—Charley Weisse, New York	KO	6

Oct.	21—Young Terry, Newark L	10
Nov.	19—Tom Chester, New York .... KO	6
Dec.	20—Jackie Ennis, New York .... KO	1
1936		
Jan.	7—Jackie Aldare, New York .... KO	5
Jan.	17—Oscar Rankins, New York L	8
Mar.	3—Mickey Bottone, New York .... KO	1
Mar.	9—Young Terry, Newark .... KO	7
Mar.	30—Roscoe Manning, Newark .... D	10
Apr.	21—Jose Pimental, New York .... KO	4
Apr.	27—Anson Green, Pittsburgh .... KO	8
May	25—Al Quaill, Pittsburgh L	10
June	15—Joe Spiegel, Pittsburgh .... KO	6
June	22—Johnny Rossi, Pittsburgh .... KO	5
Sept.	8—Ralph Chong, New York .... KO	7
Sept.	21—Frank Battaglia, Pittsburgh ...... W	10
Oct.	6—John Anderson, New York .... W	10
Oct.	22—Oscar Rankins, Pittsburgh .... W	12
Nov.	17—Roscoe Manning, New York ...... W	10
Dec.	16—Harry Balsamo, New York ...... KO	7
1937		
Jan.	13—Teddy Yarosz, New York L	10
Feb.	2—Bob Turner, New York .... KO	7
Feb.	17—Fred Apostoli, New York L	10
Mar.	18—Oscar Rankins, Pittsburgh L	10
Apr.	4—Eddie McGuire, New York ..... KO	4
Apr.	14—Fred Apostoli, New York ..... KO by	5
Aug.	12—Walter Woods, New York .... KO	8
Aug.	21—Joe Ducca, Brooklyn .... KO	6
Oct.	3—Walter Woods, New York L	10
Oct.	27—Eddie Maguire, New York .... KO	7
Nov.	17—Frank Battaglia, New York ...... W	10
Dec.	16—Billy Conn, Pittsburgh .... W	12
1938		
Jan.	1—George Black .... KO	3
Jan.	25—Al Diamond, Brooklyn .... KO	1
Feb.	9—Johnny Rossi, New York .... KO	4
Mar.	8—Stanley Hasrato, New York ...... KO	7
Apr.	6—Izzy Jannazzo, New York .... KO	11
May	20—Glen Lee, New York L	10
June	14—Freddie Steele, Seattle L	10
July	15—Swede Berglund, Hollywood ..... KO	6
Aug.	10—Ace of Spades, Oakland .... KO	4
Aug.	24—Dale Sparr, Oakland .... KO	6
Nov.	1—Al Hostak, Seattle .... W	15
	(Won NBA Middleweight Title)	
Nov.	28—Billy Conn, Pittsburgh L	12
Dec.	5—Carmen Barth, Cleveland .... W	10
Dec.	16—Red Farmer, San Francisco .... KO	8
1939		
Jan.	2—Marty Simmons, Milwaukee .... D	10
Feb.	23—Ben Brown, Miami .... KO	9
Apr.	5—Allen Matthews, Seattle .... W	10
May	12—Billy Conn, New York L	12
June	27—Al Hostak, Seattle .... KO by	4
	(Lost NBA Middleweight Title)	
1940		
Feb.	3—Texas Joe Dundee, Brooklyn ...... KO	3
Feb.	17—Mario Liani, Brooklyn .... KO	5
Apr.	23—Herbie Katz, Brooklyn .... KO	4
May	16—Jimmy Reeves, Cleveland L	10

95

July	1—Al McCoy, Woodhaven .... W	10
July	18—Carl Johnson, Brooklyn .... KO	4
Aug.	12—Wally Sears, Woodhaven .... KO	3
Nov.	1—Tommy Tucker, New York L	8
Dec.	17—Melio Bettina, Brooklyn L	10

1941

Mar.	10—Pat Valentino, San Francisco L	10
May	13—Dan Gill, Los Angeles .... KO	6
May	28—Booker Beckwith, Chicago L	10
July	22—Lee Savold, Brooklyn L	10

TB	KO	WD	WF	D	LD	LF	KO BY	ND	NC
112	54	27	0	7	21	0	3	0	0

TONY ZALE
(Anthony Florian Zaleski)
(The Man of Steel)
Born, May 29, 1913, Gary Indiana. Weight, 160
lbs. Height, 5 ft. 8 in. Managed by Sam Pian and Art
Winch.

1934

June	11—Eddie Allen, Chicago	W	4
June	15—Johnny Simpson, Chicago	W	4
June	21—Bobby Millsap, Chicago	KO	1
June	25—Johnny Liston, Chicago	KO	3
July	2—Ossie Jefferson, Chicago	KO	3
July	9—Lou Bartell, Chicago	W	4
July	16—Einar Headquist, Chicago	KO	4
July	30—Bobby Millsap, Chicago	W	4
Aug.	6—Bruce Wade, Peoria	KO	2
Aug.	13—Billy Hood, Chicago	L	6
Aug.	20—George Black, Chicago	L	6
Aug.	27—Wilbur Stokes, Chicago	W	8
Sept.	3—Mickey Misko, Chicago	L	8
Sept.	17—Mickey Misko, Chicago	KO	4
Oct.	8—Jack Blackburn, Chicago	W	8
Oct.	19—Jackie Schwartz, Milwaukee	KO	4
Oct.	22—Frankie Misko, Chicago	KO	6
Oct.	28—Jackie Schwartz, Milwaukee	KO	4
Nov.	5—Jack Charvez, Chicago	W	8
Nov.	26—Kid Leonard, Peoria	L	10
Dec.	17—Jack Gibbons, Chicago	L	10
Dec.	28—Joey Bazzone, Chicago	L	6

1935

Jan.	7—Max Elling, Chicago	W	8
Feb.	4—Joe Bazzone, Chicago	L	6
Feb.	11—Roughhouse Glover, Cincinnati	KO	9
Feb.	25—Jack Blackburn, Chicago	W	6
Mar.	11—Max Elling, Chicago	W	8
May	6—Johnny Phagan, Chicago	KO by	6
July	2—Dave Clark, Chicago	L	6

1936

Apr.	13—Jack Moran, Chicago	D	5

1937

July	26—Elby Johnson, Chicago	W	4
Sept.	17—Elby Johnson, Chicago	KO	3
Oct.	11—Billy Brown, Chicago	KO	1
Oct.	18—Bobby Gerry, Chicago	KO	2
Nov.	1—Nate Bolden, Chicago	L	5
Nov.	22—Nate Bolden, Chicago	W	6
Dec.	2—Leon Jackson, Gary	W	6

1938

Jan.	3—Nate Bolden, Chicago	W	8
Jan.	24—Henry Schaft, Chicago	W	8
Feb.	21—Jimmy Clark, Chicago	KO by	1
Mar.	28—King Wyatt, Chicago	W	8
May	16—Bobby LaMonte, Chicago	W	5
June	13—Jimmy Clark, Chicago	KO	8
July	18—Billy Celebron, Chicago	D	10
Aug.	17—Manual Davila, Chicago	L	4
Aug.	22—Billy Celebron, Chicago	L	10
Oct.	10—Tony Cisco, Chicago	W	10
Oct.	31—Jimmy Clark, Chicago	KO	2
Nov.	18—Enzo Iannozzi, Chicago	W	6

1939

Jan.	2—Nate Bolden, Chicago	L	10
May	1—Johnny Shaw, Chicago	KO	5
May	23—Babe Orgovan, New York	W	6
Aug.	14—Milton Shivers, Chicago	KO	3
Oct.	6—Sherman Edwards, Chicago	KO	3
Nov.	3—Al Wardlow,1 Youngstown	KO	3
Nov.	11—Eddie Mileski, Chicago	KO	1
Dec.	12—Babe Orgovan, Chicago	KO	3

1940

Jan.	29—Al Hostak, Chicago	W	10
Feb.	29—Enzo Iannozzi Youngstown	KO	4
Mar.	29—Ben Brown, Chicago	KO	3
June	12—Baby Kid Chocolate, Youngstown .	KO	4
July	19—Al Hostak, Seattle	KO	13
	(Won NBA Middleweight Title)		
Aug.	21—Billy Soost, Chicago	L	10
Nov.	19—Fred Apostoli, Seattle	W	10

1941

Jan.	1—Tony Martin, Milwaukee	KO	8
Jan.	10—Steve Mamakos, Chicago	W	10
Feb.	21—Steve Mamakos, Chicago	KO	14
	(Retained NBA Middleweight Title)		
May	28—Al Hostak, Chicago	KO	2
	(Retained NBA Middleweight Title)		
July	23—Ossie Harris, Chicago	KO	1
Aug.	16—Billy Pryor, Milwaukee	KO	9
Nov.	28—Georgie Abrams, New York	W	15
	Won Vacant World Middleweight Title)		

1942

Feb.	13—Billy Conn, New York	L	12

1943-1945
(Inactive)

1946

Jan.	7—Bobby Giles, Kansas City	KO	4
Jan.	17—Tony Gillo, Norfolk	KO	5
Feb.	7—Oscar Boyd, Des Moines	KO	3
Feb.	26—Bobby Claus, Houston	KO	4
Apr.	12—Ira Hughes, Houston	KO	2
May	2—Eddie Rossi, Memphis	KO	4
Sept.	27—Rocky Graziano, New York	KO	6
	(Retained World Middleweight Title)		

1947

Feb.	3—Deacon Logan, Omaha	KO	6
Feb.	12—Len Wadsworth, Wichta	KO	3
Mar.	20—Tommy Charles, Memphis	KO	4
Apr.	1—Al Timmons, Kansas City	KO	5
May	8—Cliff Beckett, Youngstown	KO	6
July	16—Rocky Graziano, Chicago	KO by	6
	(Lost World Middleweight Title)		

1948

Jan.	23—Al Turner, Grand Rapids	KO	5
Mar.	8—Bobby Claus, Little Rock	KO	4
Mar.	19—Lou Woods, Toledo	KO	3
June	10—Rocky Graziano, Newark	KO	3
	(Regained World Middleweight Title)		
Sept.	21—Marcel Cerdan Jersey City	KO by	12
	(Lost World Middleweight Title)		

TB	KO	WD	WF	D	LD	LF	KO BY	ND	NC
90	46	24	0	2	14	0	4	0	0

Elected to Boxing Hall of Fame, 1958.

YOUNG CORBETT III

(Rafelle Capabianca Giordano)
Born, May 27, 1905, Protenza, Campania, Italy
Weight, 126-160 lbs Height, 5 ft 7½ in Managed by
Ralph Manfredo, Larry White

1919

Oct.	3—Kid Jeffries, Fresno	D	4

1920

Feb.	5—Eddie Morris, Marysville	KO by	3
June	18—Terry Hogan, Fresno	D	4
July	1—Terry Hogan, Fresno	W	4
July	3—Kid Chris, Fresno	W	4
July	23—Kid Chris, Fresno	KO	2
Aug.	17—Eddie Mahoney, Fresno	W	4
Sept.	28—Young Terry McGovern, Fresno	W	4
Nov.	23—Young Battling Nelson, Fresno	W	4

1921

Jan.	10—Young Peters, Porterville	W	4
Sept.	27—Young Terry McGovern, Fresno	L	4
Dec.	15—Kid Hardy, Tulare	D	4

1922

Oct.	24—Red Santos, Tulare	D	4

1923

Jan.	9—Billy Jordan, Fresno	KO	2
Jan.	23—Billy Cole, Fresno	KO	2
Feb.	6—Jimmy Brady, Fresno	W	4
Feb.	9—Lee Weber, Hanford	W	4
Feb.	16—Pat Ryan, Tulare	KO	1
Apr.	19—Clarence Sanchez, Hanford	W	4
Apr.	26—Joe Simas, Tulare	W	4
May	10—Kid Hudson, Hanford	KO	2
May	22—Lee Weber, Tulare	W	4
June	28—Eddie Mahoney, Visalia	W	4
July	26—Ad Ramey, Visalia	W	4
Aug.	31—Kid Paeloff, Bakersfield	KO	2
Sept.	14—Kid Ritchie, Bakersfield	D	4
Sept.	18—Young Pardella, Fresno	W	4
Oct.	16—Frankie Vierra, Fresno	W	4
Oct.	31—Georgie Lee, Fresno	W	4
Nov.	9—Tommy O'Leary, Sacramento	W	4
Nov.	20—Eddie Haddon, Fresno	W	4
Dec.	29—Trench King, Fresno	L	4

1924

Feb.	17—Joe Bell, Merced	W	4
Mar.	4—Benny Berries, Fresno	W	4
Mar.	17—Joe Chaney, Tulare	D	4
Apr.	8—Benny Berries, Fresno	D	4
Apr.	21—Battling Triego, Bakersfield	W	4
Apr.	28—Kid Swan, Bakersfield	KO	2
May	2—Jack Sparr, Hollywood	W	4
May	9—Sailor Ad Cadena, San Pedro	L	4
May	27—K. O. Kelly, Vernon	L	4
Sept.	24—Pete Francis, Hanford	W	4
Nov.	11—Joe Chaney, Exeter	W	4
Nov.	18—Julie Jessick, Fresno	D	4
Dec.	16—Indian Mike Doyle, Fresno	W	4

1925

Feb.	6—Julie Jessick, Fresno	D	6
Mar.	11—Gilbert Gallant, Hanford	KO	2
Mar.	24—Dominic Jack McCarthy, Fresno	L	10
Apr.	27—Kid Kopecks, Fresno	KO	6
June	19—Young Sam Langford, Bakersfield	D	10

99

July	7—Joe Powell, Fresno	W	8
Aug.	7—Billy Rayes, Taft	W	6
Aug.	21—Ernie Goozeman, Taft	W	8
Oct.	27—Jack Garcia, Bakersfield	KO	5

1926

Jan.	11—Sailor Carter, Fresno	KO	5
Jan.	25—Battling Ward, Taft	W	10
Feb.	19—Dick Hoppe, Bakersfield	W	8
Feb.	23—Young Freeman, Fresno	KO	3
Apr.	23—Sammy Robideau, San Pedro	D	10
May	10—Danny McCoy, Taft	KO	4
May	18—Young Jack Thompson, Fresno	W	6
May	25—Young Burmay, Taft	KO	6
June	15—Joe Schlocker, Fresno	W	10
June	24—Jack Sparr, Fresno	W	10
June	29—Frankie Thomas, Fresno	W	6
July	5—Billy Alger, Pismo Beach	D	10
July	13—Young Papke, Fresno	W	10
July	26—Leo Claro, Taft	KO	4
Aug.	6—Billy Alger, San Diego	W	10
Aug.	27—Joe Layman, San Diego	W	10
Sept.	10—Sailor Ashmore, Taft	KO	5
Sept.	24—Charley Feraci, San Diego	W	10
Oct.	5—Jerry Carpentero, Fresno	KO	6
Oct.	12—Joe Chaney, Tulare	W	6
Nov.	3—Jack Sparr, Fresno	KO	3
Nov.	23—Sailor Ashmore, Fresno	KO	3
Dec.	3—Dick Hoppe, Hollywood	W	10

1927

Jan	18—Phil Salvadore, Fresno	KO	4
Mar.	1—Larry Murphy, Fresno	W	10
Mar.	23—Billy Murphy, Oakland	D	10
Apr.	13—Young Harry Wills, Oakland	WF	10
May	25—Frankie Tierney, Oakland	W	10
June	7—Jack Silver, Fresno	W	10
June	24—Young Jack Thompson, San Francisco	D	10
July	29—Tommy White, San Francisco	D	10
Aug.	5—Freddie Mack, San Francisco	W	10
Sept.	20—Joe Vargas, Fresno	W	10
Oct.	21—Charley Feraci, San Diego	W	10
Nov.	1—Dave Cook, Fresno	KO	2
Dec.	14—Gilbert Attell, San Francisco	KO	5
Dec.	21—Young Sam Langford, San Francisco	W	10

1928

Feb.	13—Young Jack Thompson, San Francisco	W	10
Mar.	12—K. O. Eddie Roberts, San Francisco	KO	9
Apr.	20—Tony Azevedo, Hanford	W	10
June	18—Jack Zivic, San Francisco	W	10
Aug.	17—Nick Testo, San Francisco	KO	5
Sept.	13—Sgt. Sammy Baker, New York	W	12
Sept.	26—Sgt. Sammy Baker, Brooklyn	L	12

1929

Jan.	11—Pete Meyers, San Francisco	D	10
Feb.	12—Al Gracio, San Francisco	KO	7
Mar.	15—Fred Mahan, San Francisco	W	10
Apr.	22—Pete Meyers, San Francisco	W	10
June	7—Al Van Ryan, San Francisco	W	10
June	22—Clyde Chastain, San Francisco	W	10
Aug.	30—Bucky Lawless, San Francisco	KO	1

Dec.	13—Tommy Elks, San Francisco	W	10

1930

Jan.	1—Babe Anderson, San Jose	W	10
Feb.	22—Jackie Fields, San Francisco	W	10
Apr.	25—Alf Ros, San Francisco	W	10
May	16—Andy DiVodi, San Francisco	KO	4
July	4—Young Jack Thompson, San Francisco	W	10
Oct.	1—Sammy Jackson, Los Angeles	W	10
Nov.	5—Farmer Joe Cooper, Oakland	KO	1

1931

Jan.	13—Paulie Walker, Los Angeles	D	10
Feb.	20—Paulie Walker, San Francisco	W	10
Mar.	20—Paul Pirrone, San Francisco	W	10
May	1—Tommy Herman, San Francisco	W	10
June	18—Meyer Grace, Hollywood	W	10
Aug.	14—Gaston LeCadre, San Francisco	W	10

1932

Mar.	4—David Velasco, San Francisco	W	10
Apr.	12—Ceferino Garcia, Los Angeles	W	10
Apr.	21—David Velasco, Sacramento	W	10
May	16—Vearl Whitehead, San Francisco ...	W	10
June	9—Lou Savin, Alameda	Exh.	4
Aug.	19—Babe Anderson, Stockton	KO	9
Oct.	25—Ceferino Garcia, Fresno	W	10
Dec.	19—Joe Glick, San Francisco	W	10

1933

Feb.	22—Jack Fields, San Francisco	W	10
	(Won World Welterweight Title)		
May	29—Jimmy McLarnin, Los Angeles	KO by	1
	(Lost World Welterweight Title)		

1934

Feb.	5—Babe Marino, San Francisco	W	10
Apr.	30—Young Terry, San Francisco	KO	3
Aug.	14—Mickey Walker, San Francisco	W	10

1935

Jan.	20—Bep Van Klaveren, San Francisco .	W	10
Feb.	22—Bep Van Klaveren, San Francisco ..	W-10	
July	4—Lou Brouillard, San Francisco	L	10

1936

July	1—Mike Bozzone, San Francisco	W	10
July	10—Johnny Diaz, Oakland	KO	7
Sept.	18—Joe Bernal, Fresno	W	10

1937

Mar.	12—Gus Lesnevich, San Francisco	KO	5
Apr.	2—Dale Sparr, San Francisco	W	10
July	21—Joe Smallwood, Oakland	W	10
Aug.	13—Billy Conn, San Francisco	W	10
Nov.	8—Billy Conn, Pittsburgh	L	10
Dec.	17—Dick Foster, San Francisco	W	10

1938

Feb.	22—Fred Apostoli, San Francisco	W	10
May	25—Jack Burke, Sal Lake City	W	10
July	19—Glen Lee, Fresno	W	10
No.	18—Fred Apostoli, New York	KO by	8
	(For World Middleweight Title)		

1939

Dec.	14—Dick Foster, San Francisco	KO	7

1940

Mar.	13—Dale Sparr, Oakland	W	10
Apr.	15—Harry Cahill, San Francisco	W	10

Aug. 20—Sheik Rangel, Fresno .... W 10
1941
(Inactive)
1942
Feb. 11—Homer McGrew, Fresno .... Exh. 3

TB	KO	WD	WF	D	LD	LF	KO	BY	ND	NC
151	33	89	1	17	8	0	3		0	0

MELIO BETTINA

Born, November 18, 1916, Bridgeport, Conn.
Weight, 172-180 lbs. Height, 5 ft. 10 in. Managed by
James V. Grippo.

1934

Oct.	6—Joe Gargiso, New York	KO	1
Oct.	27—John Dario, New York	KO	2
Nov.	10—Terry Mitchell, New York	W	4
Dec.	1—Julius Vigh, New York	KO	3

1935

Mar.	15—Jimmy Varrelli, New York	W	6
Apr.	4—Vinnie Funk, Paterson	KO	2
Apr.	11—Babe Marshall, Paterson	W	6
Apr.	22—Ray Miller, Paterson	L	6
May	2—Charlie Mautz, Paterson	W	8
June	3—Lou LaPage, Paterson	W	10
June	25—Alfie Williams, Elmira	KO	3
Sept.	10—Mark Hough, Poughkeepsie	D	8
Nov.	13—Tiger Smith, New Haven	W	6

1936

Jan.	9—Joe Tinsely, White Plains	W	6
Feb.	17—Babe Childers, Miami Beach	KO	2
Mar.	10—Tony Celli, West Palm Beach	W	10
Mar.	31—Charlie Weiss, W. Palm Beach	L	10
Apr.	14—Charlie Weiss, W. Palm Beach	W	10
June	1—Bud Mignault, Poughkeepsie	W	10
July	13—Charlie Loughran, Washington	W	6
July	27—Buddy Ryan, Newark	NC	6
Aug.	24—Fred Caruso, Newark	L	10
Sept.	14—Frank Zamoris, Newark	KO by	6
Sept.	28—Frank Zamoris, Newark	W	8
Nov.	16—Buddy Ryan, Newark	W	8
Dec.	8—Steve Carr, West Palm Beach	KO	6

1937

Jan.	12—Carl Knowles, W. Palm Beach	KO	3
Jan.	26—Leroy Brown, W. Palm Beach	D	10
Mar.	2—Tony Celli, West Palm Beach	W	10
Mar.	30—Barney Brock, Miami	W	10
June	18—Joe Knight, Miami	W	10
July	10—Jimmy Mendes, Bridgeport	KO	5
July	24—Joe Lipps, Bridgeport	KO	5
Aug.	7—Johnny Duarte, Bridgeport	W	8
Aug.	20—Buck Everett, Miami Beach	L	10
Sept.	28—Art Johnson, Los Angeles	KO	4
Nov.	5—Swede Berglund, Hollywood	W	10
Dec.	10—Swede Berglund, Hollywood	KO	3

1938

Feb.	4—Bob Godwin, West Palm Beach	KO	7
Mar.	11—Tony Celli, West Palm Beach	KO	2
Mar.	25—Pat McDuff, West Palm Beach	W	10
May	5—James J. Johnson, New York	KO	7
May	20—Dominic Ceccarelli; New York	W	6
June	17—Phil Sommese, Brooklyn	W	10
July	2—John Lasinski, Milford	KO	5
July	26—Gene Bonin, Poughkeepsie	KO	2
Aug.	18—Buck Everett, Poughkeepsie	KO	1
Oct.	10—Basher Dean, Plainfield	W	8

1939

Jan.	3—Bud Mignault, New York	....	KO	10
Jan.	20—Henry Cooper, New York	....	W	8
Feb.	3—Tiger Jack Fox, New York	....	KO	9

(Won Vacant New York World Light Heavyweight Title)

| May | 15—Italo Colonello, Pittsburgh | .... | KO | 3 |
| July | 13—Billy Conn, New York | .... | L | 15 |

(For Vacant World Light Heavyweight Title)

| Aug. | 8—Hobo Williams, Poughkeepsie | ..... | W | 8 |
| Sept. | 25—Billy Conn, Pittsburgh | .... | L | 15 |

(For World Light Heavyweight Title)

| Nov. | 28—Willie Pavlovich, Jersey City | ...... | W | 8 |
| Dec. | 15—Mario Liani, Kingston | .... | KO | 4 |

1940

Jan.	5—Fred Apostoli, New York	....	L	12
Feb.	2—Fred Apostoli, New York	....	KO	12
June	7—Al McCoy, Boston	....	L	10
Aug.	7—Joe O'Gatty, Amsterdam	....	W	10
Sept.	10—Gunnar Barlund, New York	....	W	10
Dec.	17—Solly Krieger, Brooklyn	....	W	10

1941

| Jan. | 13—Anton Christoforidis, Cleveland | .... | L | 15 |

(For Vacant NBA Light Heavyweight Title)

Feb.	21—Herbie Katz, New York	....	KO	9
Mar.	9—Buddy Knox, Miami	....	KO	5
Mar.	25—Jack Marshall, Tampa	....	KO	9
July	22—Red Burman, Brooklyn	....	W	10
Aug.	25—Pat Valentino, San Francisco	......	W	10
Oct.	7—Sonny Boy Walker, Los Angeles	...	W	10
Nov.	17—Jimmy Bivins, Cleveland	....	W	10
Dec.	1—Harry Bobo, Pittsburgh	....	W	10

1942

Jan.	12—Mose Brown, Pittsburgh	....	W	10
Mar.	31—Gus Dorazio, Philadelphia	....	W	10
Apr.	10—Booker Beckwith, Chicago	....	W	10
June	12—Altus Allen, Chicago	....	W	10
June	23—Harry Bobo, Cleveland	....	W	10

1943

| June | 14—Lou Brooks, Philadelphia | .... | KO | 1 |
| Sept. | 15—Jimmy Bivins, Cleveland | .... | L | 10 |

1944

May	22—Johnny Vorce, Pittsburgh	....	KO	5
June	12—Buddy Walker, Pittsburgh	....	W	10
July	18—Curtis Sheppard, Pittsburgh	....	W	10
Oct.	16—Saint Thomas, Philadelphia	......	KO	3
Dec.	11—George Parks, Washington, D.C.	...	W	10

1945

| Mar. | 16—Jimmy Bivins, New York | .... | D | 10 |

1946

July	11—Eddie Blunt, Hartford	....	W	10
Aug.	19—Larry Bouchard, Troy	....	KO	2
Sept.	25—Eldridge Eatman, Norwalk	....	W	10
Nov.	19—Bill Weinberg, Buffalo	....	W	10
Dec.	10—Joe Muscato, Buffalo	....	KO	3

1947

| May | 23—Gus Lesnevich, New York | ..... | KO by | 1 |

1948

May	12—Jackie Fisher, Bangor, Me.	....	KO	5
May	24—Ross Strickland, Newburgh	....	KO	5
June	16—Angel Sotillo, New york	....	KO	3

```
July     6—Austin Johnson, Elizabeth ........ KO    2
July    27—Shamus O'Brien, New York ...... KO    4
Nov.     8—Sandy McPherson, Providence ..... W   10
Nov.    19—Enrique Felipi, New York ......... W   10
Dec.    21—Johnny Flynn, Rochester ...... KO by   6
```

TB	KO	WD	WF	D	LD	LF	KO BY	ND	NC
99	36	46	0	3	10	0	3	0	1

GUS LESNEVICH

Born, February 22, 1915, Cliffside Park, N.J.
Weight, 175 lbs. Height, 5 ft. 9 in. Managed by lou
Diamond, Joe Vella.

1934

May	5—Justin Hoffman, Brooklyn	KO	2
May	19—Sid Cohen, Brooklyn	KO	3
May	29—Jimmy Calabrese, Ft. Lee	KO	1
June	9—Willie Kline, Brooklyn	W	6
June	16—Roy Frisco, Brooklyn	W	8
July	23—Tony Calabrese, Jersey City	KO	2
Sept.	13—Nicky Williams, Teterboro	W	6
Sept.	22—Charlie Weisse, Brooklyn	W	6
Oct.	3—Mark Hough, Brooklyn	W	6
Nov.	3—Tom Chester, Brooklyn	W	6
Nov.	24—Jackie Aldare, Brooklyn	L	6
Dec.	8—Stan Willardson, Brooklyn	W	6
Dec.	29—Jackie Adare, Brooklyn	W	8

1935

Jan.	12—Bucky Lawless, Brooklyn	KO	2
Feb.	2—Jackie Aldare, Brooklyn	W	8
Mar.	2—John Anderson, Brooklyn	W	8
Mar.	22—John Anderson, New York	D	8
Apr.	13—Mark Hough, Brooklyn	W	8
May	4—Tom Chester, Brooklyn	W	8
May	25—Tony Celli, Brooklyn	W	8
Dec.	17—Butch Lynch, Newark	W	10

1936

Jan.	—Billy Hood, Miami	W	6
Feb.	4—Eddie Whalen, Jersey City	KO	5
Mar.	16—Frankie Caris, Newark	D	10
Apr.	13—Frankie Caris, Newark	W	10
May	19—Sammy Christian, Los Angeles	W	4
May	29—Johnny Sykes, Hollywood	KO	1
June	19—Lou Rogers, Hollywood	KO	1
Aug.	21—Ray Actis, Hollywood	W	10
Oct.	9—Carmen Barth, Hollywood	W	10
Oct.	23—Marty Simmions, Hollywood	D	10
Nov.	4—Young Stuhley, San Francisco	KO	9
Nov.	17—Freddie Steele, Los Angeles	KO by	2

1937

Feb.	20—Tony Celli, New York	W	8
Mar.	12—Young Corbett III, San Francisco	KO by	5
May	14—Johnny Romero, Hollywood	KO	7
June	22—Young Stuhley, Los Angeles	W	10
Aug.	24—Atilio Sabatino, Los Angeles	W	10
Sept.	3—Alabama Kid, San Francisco	W	10

Oct.	5—Allen Matthews, Seattle	D	10
Nov.	19—Herbie Katz, New York	W	8

1938

Jan.	7—Joey Parks, St. Louis	D	10
Feb.	8—Ben Brown, Coral Gables	W	10
Feb.	24—Jack Kirkland, Miami Beach	KO	1
Mar.	23—Lou Brouillard, New York	W	10
June	1—Buddy Ryan, West New York	W	10
June	16—Stanley Hasrato, West New York	KO	1
Oct.	27—Ron Richards, Sydney	L	15
Dec.	6—Ambrose Palmer, Sydney	W	15

106

1939

Jan.	19—Alabama Kid, Sydney	KO	9
Feb.	2—Bob Olin, Sydney	W	12
May	15—Larry Lane, Trenton	W	10
June	22—Dave Clark, Nutley	KO	1
Nov.	17—Billy Conn, New York	L	15

(For World Light Heavyweight Title)

1940

Jan.	1—Dave Clark, Detroit	W	10
June	5—Billy Conn, Detroit	L	15

(For World Light Heavyweight Title)

July	22—Wally Sears, Garfield	W	10
Sept.	5—Henry Cooper, Garfield	KO	5
Nov.	23—Al Delaney, Brooklyn	L	10
Dec.	16—Jack Marshall, Newark	KO	4

1941

Feb.	27—Nathan Mann, Detroit	W	10
May	22—Anton Christoforidis, New York ...	W	15

(Won NBA Light Heavyweight Title)

Aug.	26—Tami Mauriello, New York	W	15

(Won Vacant World Light Heavyweight Title)

Nov.	14—Tami Mauriello, New York	W	15

(Retained World Light Heavyweight Title)

1942

Jan.	30—Bob Pastor, New York	L	10
Mar.	11—Jimmy Bivins, Cleveland	L	10

1943

Oct.	22—Joe Thomas, Wilmington .... Exh.	KO	3

1944-1945
(Inactive)

1946

Jan.	11—Joe Kahut, Portland, Ore.	KO	1
Feb.	15—Paul Crosby, Danbury, Conn. .... Exh.		5
Feb.	22—Lee Oma, New York	KO by	4
May	14—Freddie Mills, London	KO	10

(Retained World Light Heavyweight Title)

Sept.	17—Bruce Woodcock, London	KO by	8

1947

Feb.	28—Billy Fox, New York	KO	10

(Retained World Light Heavyweight Title)

May	23—Melio Bettina, New York	KO	1
July	30—Tami Mauriello, Brooklyn	W	10
Oct.	31—Tami Mauriello, New York	KO	7

1948

Mar.	5—Billy Fox, New York	KO	1

(Retained World Light Heavyweight Title)

July	26—Freddie Mills, London	L	15

(Lost World Light Heavyweight Title)

1949

Mar.	3—Eldridge Eatman, Newark	KO	1
May	23—Joey Maxim, Cincinnati	L	15

(For Vacant American Light Heavyweight Title)

Aug.	10—Ezzard Charles, New York .... KO by		7

(For NBA Heavyweight Title)

TB	KO	WD	WF	D	LD	LF	KO BY	ND	NC
79	23	37	0	5	9	0	5	0	0

Died, February 28, 1964. Cliffside Park, N.J.
Elected to Boxing Hall of Fame, 1973.

FRED APOSTOLI

Born, February 2, 1913, San Francisco, Calif.
Weight, 160 lbs. Height, 5 ft. 7 in. Managed by Harold
Seadron.

1934 National AAU Middleweight Champion

1934

Oct.	8—Gilbert Attell, San Francisco . . . . . KO	3
Nov.	12—Jack Riley, San Francisco . . . . KO	1
Nov.	30—Eddie Daniels, San Francisco : . . . . KO	2

1935

Jan.	7—Eddie Fox, San Francisco . . . . KO	5
Jan.	28—Andy DiVodi, San Francisco . . . . . . W	6
Feb.	22—Newsboy Millich, San Francisco . . KO	4
Apr.	1—Freddie Steele, San Francisco . . KO by	10
May	31—Mike Payan, San Francisco . . . . W	10
July	17—Eddie Schneider, San Francisco . . . KO	1
July	31—Dick Foster, San Francisco . . . . . . KO	6
Aug.	14—Rudy Mendez, San Francisco . . . . . W	8
Oct.	4—Young Stuhley, San Francisco , . . . W	10
Oct.	25—Babe Marino, San Francisco . . . . . . W	10
Nov.	27—Swede Berglund, San Francisco . . . . W	10

1936

Jan.	20—Frankie Britt, San Francisco . . . . . . W	10
Feb.	28—Paul Pirrone, San Francisco . . . . . . KO	7
Apr.	6—Young Stuhley, San Francisco . . . . . W	10
May	8—Babe Risko, San Francisco . . . . W	10
Aug.	21—Marty Simmons, San Francisco . . . . W	10
Oct.	9—Lou Brouillard, San Francisco . . . . . W	10
Dec.	14—Babe Marino, San Francisco . . . . W	10

1937

Jan.	27—Ken Overlin, New York L	10
Feb.	17—Solly Krieger, New York . . . . W	10
Mar.	15—Joe (Butch) Lynch, Newark . . . . KO	9
Apr.	14—Solly Krieger, New York . . . . KO	5
June	11—Dale Sparr, San Francisco . . . . W	10
June	22—Tommy Jones, Portland, Ore. . . . . . KO	2
Sept.	23—Marcel Thil, New York . . . . KO	10
	(Won World Middleweight Title)	
Oct.	25—Tony Celli, Philadelphia . . . . KO	2

1938

Jan.	7—Freddie Steele, New York . . . . KO	9
Feb.	4—Glen Lee, New York . . . . W	12
Feb.	22—Young Corbett III, San Francisco . . . L	10
Apr.	1—Glen Lee, New York . . . . W	15
	(Retained World Middleweight Title)	
Sept.	6—Mike Payan, San Jose, Calif. . . . . . KO	10
Sept.	16—Joe (Butch) Lynch, San Francisco . KO	2
Nov.	18—Young Corbett III, New York . . . . . KO	8
	(Retained World Middleweight Title)	
Dec.	20—Al Cocozza, New Haven . . . . KO	4

1939

Jan.	6—Billy Conn, New York L	10
Feb.	10—Billy Conn, New York L	15
Apr.	17—George Nichols, Houston . . . . KO	2
May	11—Eric Seelig, Cleveland . . . . W	10
Aug.	7—Mohammed Fahmy, Springfield . . . KO	3
Aug.	28—Glen Lee, Pittsburgh . . . . W	10
Oct.	2—Ceferino Garcia, New York . . . . KO by	7
	(Lost World Middleweight Title)	

108

1940

Jan.	5—Melio Bettina, New York	W	12
Feb.	2—Melio Bettina, New York	KO by	12
	—Freddie Graham, San Francisco .	Exh.	4
July	22—Dale Sparr, San Francisco	KO	2
Aug.	19—Big Boy Hogue, San Francisco	W	10
Sept.	16—Bobby Pacho, San Francisco	W	10
Nov.	19—Tony Zale, Seattle	L	10

1941

Aug.	21—Bill McDowell, Norfolk, Va.	KO	2
Sept.	15—Joey Spangler, Norfolk, Va.	KO	5
Oct.	14—Ed Brookman, Washington, D.C. ...	KO	6

1942

Mar.	7—Augie Arellano, Brooklyn	KO	5
Apr.	4—Joe Mulli, Brooklyn	KO	1
June	26—Ken Overlin, Norfolk, Va.	D	10
Aug.	24—Saverio Turiello, Norfolk, Va.	W	10

1943
(Inactive)

1944

May	26—Vic Grupico, San Francisco	Exh.	4

1945
(Inactive)

1946

Aug.	12—Pedro Jiminez, San Francisco	KO	4
Aug.	27—Sheik Rangel, Sacramento	W	10
Sept.	9—Dencio Cabanella, San Francisco .	KO	7
Sept.	20—George Duke, San Francisco	KO	9
Oct.	21—Tommy Egan, San Francisco	W	10
Nov.	18—Frank Angustain, San Francisco ...	W	10
Dec.	11—Paul Lewis, Oakland, Calif.	W	10

1947

Feb.	28—Bobby Volk, San Francisco	KO by	1
Apr.	7—Bobby Volk, San Francisco	KO	3
May	2—George Duke, Los Manos, Calif. ...	W	10
May	21—Earl Turner, Oakland, Calif.	W	10
July	14—Reuben Shank, San Francisco	KO	8
Aug.	25—Reuben Shank, San Francisco	W	10
Nov.	17—Georgie Abrams, San Francisco	W	10

1948

Dec.	1—Earl Turner, Oakland, Calif.	L	10

TB	KO	WD	WF	D	LD	LF	KO BY	ND	NC
72	31	30	0	1	6	0	4	0	0

Died, November 29, 1973, San Francisco, Calif.
Elected to Boxing Hall of Fame, 1978.